· · · · · · · COOKBOOKS CONSIST OF LIMITED WORDS.

COOKS POSSESS UNLIMITED TALENT · · · · · · ·

點心食譜

周蘭真 著

FAVORITE DIM SUM

by

Lonnie Mock

ALPHA GAMMA ARTS
WALNUT CREEK, CALIFORNIA
1979

ISBN 0-941716-03-1

ORIGINAL PRINTING, 1979
SECOND PRINTING, 1980
THIRD PRINTING, 1982

ALPHA GAMMA ARTS
P. O. BOX 4671
WALNUT CREEK, CALIFORNIA 94596

TO MY FRIENDS AND STUDENTS,

with appreciation for their enthusiasm and encouragement

FOREWORD

Chinese cooking is one of the world's great cuisines. Books are now available for many regional cooking varieties including Cantonese, Mandarin, Szechwan and even that of Hunan. The art of dim sum cooking has not been described comprehensively and is therefore less well known to the American public. Outside of the cities with large Chinese communities, dim sum is not available and virtually unknown. Therefore there are many of us who have never savored this delicious and special variety of the Cantonese cuisine.

Lonnie Mock has performed a great service in the preparation of this unique dim sum cookbook. Mrs. Mock is an excellent cook and has taught dim sum cooking. She is eminently qualified to do this,

having been born in Hong Kong, spent her early childhood in Macao and was later educated at San Diego State University and at University of California, Berkeley where she majored in mathematics and education. She taught mathematics at the high school level but her great love has been cooking which she learned at an early age under the expert tutelage of her mother. Mrs. Mock later perfected her recipes with scientific and mathematical precision converting a "pinch of this and a dash of that" to quantitative kitchen measurements. Her innate curiosity has permitted her to adapt many of her recipes so that common American ingredients could be utilized without altering the authentic taste and texture.

Although interested in Chinese cooking

for many years, we had never undertaken dim sum dishes because they seemed too complicated. (Even the Chinese eat it out in special dim sum restaurants!) Recently, after having had the pleasure of taking a course in dim sum cooking given by Mrs. Mock, it became apparent that these dishes were not as complex as we thought. She leads even the novice through the successive stages to produce these delicacies and works of kitchen art. This comprehensive book now makes available to everyone the capability to prepare dim sum in his or her own kitchen. It is our pleasure to endorse this excellent book and to recommend it to anyone interested in Chinese cooking.

B. R. Gendel, M. D.
and
Rena Gendel

Walnut Creek
California

PREFACE

On page 169 of my *DIM SUM COOKBOOK*, I mentioned that I was to return to my kitchen for some more edible experiments. Yes, friends, I have done exactly that.

While *DIM SUM COOKBOOK* was written on personal experience, *FAVORITE DIM SUM* is written on personal experience combined with students' comments and suggestions. Some of the recipes in *FAVORITE DIM SUM*, at a glance, would seem complicated, but teaching experiences have taught me that although some of us are too busy to cook, we actually don't mind taking the time to prepare the so called complicated and lengthy recipes for our loved ones and occasionally to put on a show for company. Some of my students *make* time to cook a Peking duck, for instance, in between their busy working hours. There is really no such thing as a complicated recipe; the complexity lies in the unknown. Carefully read the recipe, understand the procedure, then try it once or twice. Even the most complex recipe becomes simple and easy.

FAVORITE DIM SUM is not a continuation of *DIM SUM COOKBOOK*. In other words, *DIM SUM COOKBOOK* is not a prerequisite of *FAVORITE DIM SUM*. Each is an independent edition. Each provides the preliminary information on cutting methods, cooking methods, utensils and tea. *FAVORITE DIM SUM* consists of all new selected choice recipes and the newest ideas and shapes in *dim sum*-making. Exceptions are the basic dough recipes and the *char shiu* recipe. These recipes are repeated in *FAVORITE DIM SUM* because they are as basic as ingredients. Included are also the popular *har gow*, *shiu mai*, *fun gor* and *char shiu bao*, but all these recipes have different fillings to give the dumplings a whole new exciting taste and flavor. Readers who do not own a copy of *DIM SUM COOKBOOK* will have the pleasure of learning these popular foods while readers who own both books will be delighted to try the dumplings with the new fillings. *FAVORITE DIM SUM* also contains the added feature of FANCY GARNISHES and SUGGESTED MENUS.

All the recipes in this book have been kitchen-tested and taste-tested. But, as we are well aware, we are all individuals with likes and dislikes. No matter how carefully and precisely the recipes are planned, there is always leeway for substituting one type of ingredient for another. Therefore, it is my hope that this book will serve as a guidepost, not an absolute. New and improved convenient products are coming into the market every day. We can be adventurous and creative.

Since the publication of *DIM SUM COOKBOOK*, I have met many wonderful people; each has helped me in his or her own way. To all you wonderful people, I am deeply grateful. I especially thank Nancy Haggerty, my personal editor, for her superb and discriminating assistance; my family for their understanding and support; and Dr. and Mrs. Benjamin R. Gendel, whom I deeply respect, for sharing their wisdom.

Lonnie Mock

CONTENTS

更上一層樓

INTRODUCTION

The Chinese word, *dim*, has more than ten different definitions. It can mean "small", "a period used in punctuation", "a dot or spot", "a geometric term used in mathematics", "bits and pieces", "giving instructions", "a bite", plus several other meanings. *Sum*, in Chinese, also has several distinct meanings. The most common ones are "center or central" and "the heart". It is also a partial character contained in more than 300 Chinese words!

Putting *dim* and *sum* together, we have another specific noun. Choosing the best meanings from the above definitions to suit our purpose, we can define *dim sum* as "snack foods, eaten at odd moments to please the heart". The origin of *dim sum* is difficult to determine. It is, however, mentioned in an ancient Chinese classic written during the Tang Dynasty (618-907 A.D.), an era distinguished for the invention of printing and the flourishing of Chinese art and poetry. *Dim sum* was then served as an early morning meal.

Recent years have shown an increasing popularity and tremendous interest in Chinese food and the Chinese way of cooking. Restaurants specializing in *dim sum* are unbelievably crowded. Patrons overflow onto the sidewalk. Take-out pastry shops sell out the choice pastries during the first two or three hours of business. Supply does not meet the demand. More and more Americans are discovering that *dim sum* is one of the most palatable and enjoyable aspects of Chinese cuisine.

Today *dim sum* is commonly served from 10 a.m. to 3 p.m. Chinese frequently use the expression *yum cha*, literally meaning "drink tea", to designate brunch, lunch or snack. Tea is rarely served alone. It is almost always served with some type of *dim sum*. Some restaurants make *dim sum* as their speciality. Trays and trays of dainty pastries, delicacies and desserts are carried or wheeled from table to table for their patrons' selection. The names of the *dim sum* are announced as the foods come around, making it easy to order. There is no menu to read and certainly no need to struggle with the Chinese language. One can simply point and say "That, please"! Indeed, *yum cha* is a gastronomical joy accompanied by a few moments of mental and physical relaxation. It provides "social benefits" in many ways. Family members are brought together, friendships are renewed, businesses are promoted, and romances take root--these are just a few of the side effects.

The *dim sum* category includes a variety of foods--sweet, sour and salty, large enough a selection to please everyone. Dishes are served in small quantities, usually three bite-sized pieces per plate. Fried rice and rice soup are served in small bowls. Noodle dishes, however, are generous servings. *Dim sum* foods can be served in other different ways. Some make elegant desserts, some make exquisite hors d'oeuvres, some make light suppers and some make appetizing meat or seafood dishes for dinner.

Some of us are hesitant to try exotic foods and new recipes. With this in mind, unusual recipes are designed for two or three servings to make the first adventure more inviting. Most recipes are designed for the average family or four to five servings. All recipes are easily doubled or tripled. Some salty fillings are interchangeable just as some sweet fillings are interchangeable, but each filling is particularly designated for the type of pastry or the method of cooking that yields the best possible result. Additional filling recipes are provided for selection, diversity and enjoyment.

Dim sum dining is a culinary experience; *dim sum* making is an art. With the precise directions given in this book plus a little effort and practice, *dim sum* making is as easy as pie!

CUTTING METHODS:

Chop. Cut into pieces of any shape.
Crush. Pound with flat surface of cleaver or use crusher.
Cube. Cut into 1/2", 3/4" or desired chunks.
Dice. Cut into pea-sized cubes.
Matchstick-cut. Cut into long narrow thin strips resembling matchsticks.
Mince. Chop finely.
Shred. Cut with grain into long strips. Slice strips across grain or diagonally, then cut slices into fine strips. Shred root vegetables with shredder if used for filling.
Slice. Cut with grain into long strips, then cut thinly across grain or diagonally.
Sliver. Cut into narrow thin strips similar to matchstick-cut but finer and shorter.

COOKING METHODS AND UTENSILS:

Pan-frying. Brown food on one side or both sides in

a small amount of oil, turning frequently. Temperatures vary from medium-low to medium-high. Thoroughly coat hot pan with oil. When oil is hot, add food. This helps to prevent sticking and to give food its crispness. Turning over can be a snap if the underside is properly browned. This is essential when baking thin crêpes and all types of pancakes. Leave ample room between pieces of food for expansion and easy turning.

Deep-frying. Food is immersed in hot oil and cooked to an even brown, turning or rolling frequently. Temperatures vary from medium-low to medium-high. Deep fat frying requires special attention. The following is a list of common sense pointers. Nevertheless, they are worth reminding. Some pointers apply to pan-frying, stir-frying, steaming and boiling as well.

Although any heavy deep pan can be used, a deep-fryer with a basket is probably the best. The basket provides gentle lowering of food pieces at the same time for even cooking and it is easily lifted up in case of bubbling over or excessive splattering. Fill the fryer with enough oil to cover food but not more than half full. Slowly heat oil, with basket in pan, until it reaches the desired temperature on the deep-fry thermometer. As soon as food is lowered into this hot fat, it is crusted to seal moisture in and oil out. If oil is not hot enough, food will sink to the bottom and sit, absorb excessive oil and cause scorching. Therefore, it is important that oil be at correct temperature before food is placed in it. If pastries look burning-brown on the outside and raw on the inside, oil is too hot or heat may be too high. If pastries are grease-soaked, oil is not hot enough or heat may be too low. The perfectly fried pastry is crisp outside and not oily inside. Cooking times given in recipes are approximations. It is best to test a piece for doneness. Remove cooked food immediately to rack or absorbent paper to drain. Overcooking means greasier fried food or indigestible pastries. Skim out crumbs and bring oil back to required temperature before frying another batch. Always fry a few pieces at a time to allow free flow and motion. Pat watery foods dry.

Deep-frying is a full-time job. Never leave a pot of oil on a hot stove unattended. If oil is heated to the smoking point, it can catch fire.

Never add water to burning oil in pan. If it is safe to do so, turn off heat and cover pan with the fryer lid--have the lid ready. Keep a quantity of baking soda handy to toss on kitchen fire at the base of the flames when applicable. Do not throw baking soda into deep fat fire as this can cause splattering. It is good practice to have all necessary items at hand. Turn and remove foods with a long handled utensil (if chopsticks are employed, use only long wooden ones). Turn the handles of all pots and pans away from you and use the stove on the far side. A splatter screen with a long handle can be a great aid. Above all, never permit children to cook with hot oil without supervision.

Filled pastries to be deep-fried should:

1. have a thicker crust, made with fresh flour. Stale flour, which has lost its natural oil and moisture, means crumbled dough and cracked pastries.
2. avoid oily and watery fillings.
3. be fried in fresh pure vegetable or peanut oil.
4. be at room temperature.
5. be fried as soon as they are made.
6. be covered with a splatter screen if crust cracks before fully cooked.
7. be added to oil only when oil has reached required temperature. If oil is not hot enough, pastries will be grease-soaked. Then, as the temperature rises, some delicate pastries will crack, causing oil to splatter. Maintain an even cooking heat temperature (not the oil temperature; oil temperature will drop as soon as food is added).

Stir-frying. Stir-fry can be done in a wok or in any large heavy-bottomed pot or skillet. Heat a clean and dry utensil over high heat (or at least medium-high heat) until hot. Add oil. When oil is hot, but not smoking, add ginger and/or garlic (if used in recipe); stir a few times to extract flavor. Add well drained vegetables or meat and stir briskly for the number of minutes specified in the recipe. Water should be added after the cooking has started and only when the vegetables have been well coated with oil and appear dry. Soft (or high-water content) vegetables such as *bok choy*, mung bean sprouts and shredded jicama require the addition of little or no water. Always sprinkle one to two tablespoons of water at a time. The addition of water to the hot pan will erupt into steam and sizzle, imparting to food that special pan-fried flavor. Adding water at the beginning or in a large quantity would result in boiling and in an uninteresting and watery dish. Soft vegetables and meat should be stir-fried in their naturally exuded juices if possible. Hard (or low-water content) vegetables such as lotus roots, potatoes and carrots require the addition of a small amount of water. Add 1/4 to 1/3 cup of water, depending on the quantity, to the vegetables after they have been thoroughly coated with oil and other seasonings or sauces. Cover pan and gently steam until tender. Semi-hard vegetables such as beans and peas can be stir-fried as soft vegetables or briefly steamed. Many of the cooking methods depend on the type of cutting. Shredded carrots, for instance, can be stir-fried as a soft vegetable, whereas chunk carrots must be treated as a hard vegetable. In stir-frying, all meat should be just delicately cooked and all vegetables should be tender-crisp. Never stir-fry a large quantity in a small pan all at once.

Steaming. The common Chinese method is the bamboo steamer (also known as bamboo trays or bamboo racks) situated in a wok filled with a small amount of water. Buns and dumplings or a plate of food are cooked in the bamboo steamer. Other devices can be easily assembled. Place the plate of food on wire rack in a large 12" or 14" skillet filled with water to below rack. Or, place a cylindical ring or an elevated rack (available at Oriental hardware stores) in a large pot having a domed lid, then top this high-standing rack with a 10" cake rack. Fill the pot with a small amount of water and put a plate of food, buns or tube pan on cake rack to steam. The water level should not be too high or too low. This is to prevent boiling over or drying out. Cover wok, skillet or pot, bring to a boil, start timing, and reduce heat (or as specified in recipe) to maintain a gentle boil. Cooking time given in recipes may vary.

INGREDIENTS:

All Chinese or Oriental ingredients are available at Chinese markets, other Oriental shops and increasingly at natural food stores and supermarkets. Good food comes from its quality components. It is essential to use choice and fresh ingredients. Substitute any disagreeable ingredient with a similar product or omit it from recipe if possible and necessary. It is the cook's responsibility to select agreeable and edible ingredients.

Abalone. Abalone is a seafood. Canned abalone is the easiest to use. It is already cooked. Abalones, fresh, dried or canned, are very expensive. Leftover canned abalones can be stored in refrigerator for about 10 days.

鮑魚

Almond powder. A pure white powder available in 10-oz. jars. Keep almond powder at room temperature.

杏仁霜

Bamboo shoots. Canned bamboo shoots in various sizes are available. Immerse unused shoots in water; keep in refrigerator. Change water daily to preserve freshness.

竹筍

Bean-curd cake. It is also called "soy bean curd cake" or "soy bean cake". Its texture can be firm, medium-firm, soft, very soft or fried in 4"x1-1/2" logs or bite-sized cubes.

豆腐

Brown slab sugar. This is made from white sugar and raw brown sugar. It is sold in 1 pound pack. Each block is approximately 1-1/2"x3"x1/2".

片糖

Char shiu. These glazed roasted pork strips can be purchased from Oriental delicatessens and some markets. For homemade char shiu, see recipe.

义燒

Chili oil. Its ingredients are salad oil and hot pepper. Use sparingly.

辣油

Chili sauce. A hot sauce made from red chili peppers.

辣椒醬

Chinese barbecue sauce. This sauce is made from beans, flour, soy sauce, sugar, salt and coloring. It is available in one-pound jar. Keeps well in closed jar in refrigerator.

燒烤醬

Chinese chives. These chives have flat green stalks that look more like garlic stalks than scallion stalks. They have a mild garlic flavor, adding a distinctive spicy taste to food. Chinese chives are often used in eggs, noodles and meat.

韮菜

Chinese 5-spice. This consists of ground peppercorns, anise, fennel seeds, cinnamon and cloves. It is available in small plastic bags in Oriental shops and in spice-sized jars in some supermarkets.

五香粉

Chinese sausages. There are liver sausages, beef sausages and pork sausages. For fillings and

臘腸 toppings, pork sausages are often used. Rinse sausages and pat dry before using.

雲耳 Cloud ears. A dried small ruffled grayish brown fungus. Sold in small packages in various sizes. They must be soaked, thoroughly rinsed, squeezed dry, and tough stems must be removed. The texture is slightly crunchy.

芫茜 Coriander. It is also called Chinese parsley or cilantro, used for seasoning and garnish. Buy fresh or freeze-dried (in spice-sized jars).

腐竹片 Dried bean-curd sheets. Large sheets of dried thin bean curd are available in 8"x14" flat packages. Bean-curd sheets are very crisp and fragile. Used as wrappers, in soups and in vegetarian dishes. Not to be confused with dried sweet bean curd, which comes in smaller (6"x1-1/2") sheets, and has a very different flavor (see below).

冬菇 Dried Chinese mushrooms. Different quality dried mushrooms are available in cellophane bags of various sizes. Mushrooms should be sun dried for one day before lengthy storage. To use in recipes, soak, remove stems and wash thoroughly.

果皮 Dried Chinese tangerine peel. Well-aged peels impart the best flavor. Soak to soften before using.

金針 Dried lily buds (golden needles). Dried lily buds are about 3" long with a pale gold color. Soak only until softened, pinch off hard stems and squeeze dry. Lily buds add a different unique flavor to steamed chicken, vegetarian foods and other dishes.

蝦米 Dried shrimp. Cooked, salted, shelled and dried shrimp is a favorite ingredient added to fillings and toppings. Soak to soften, pick over and rinse well before using.

二竹片 Dried sweet bean curd. Dried bean curd made into 6"x1-1/2" flat sheets. Frequently used in vegetarian dishes. This is not to be confused with very large (about 14"x8") sheets of dried bean curd (see above).

魚露 Fish sauce. An extract from fresh fish, contains salt, derived proteins and water. It is a thin sauce. Available in different sized bottles.

Fun (rice noodles). Fresh fun can be purchased from pastry shops. Dried and packaged fresh fun are

粉 available in Chinese markets. See recipe for homemade *fun*.

糯米 Glutinous rice. This is often labeled as sweet rice. It is a short-grain rice, sticky, used for fried rice, pastries and stuffings.

糯粉 Glutinous rice flour. Flour made from glutinous rice. It is available in one-pound packages and sometimes labeled as sweet rice flour. Sift all *imported* flours and starches.

綠豆粉 Green bean powder. Flour milled from green beans. Available in 1-lb. package.

磨原豉 Ground bean sauce. This sauce is made from yellow beans, flour, salt and water. Available in 16-oz. cans. It keeps well in closed jar in refrigerator.

猪肉 Ground pork. Over-the-counter ground pork contains too much fat. It is better to buy a piece of boneless pork, trim off some fat, cut into small strips, partially freeze until firm, but not solid, then grind. To chop with the Chinese cleaver or food processor, omit freezing. It takes only seconds to mince in the food processor.

海鮮醬 Hoisin sauce. Its ingredients are yellow beans, salt, flour, sugar, vinegar and food color. Available in 16-oz. cans. It keeps well in closed glass jar under refrigeration.

辣豆瓣醬 Hot bean sauce. A spicy thick sauce made from beans, red chili and spices.

辣醬 Hot sauce. It is made from fresh ripe red peppers, vinegar and salt. Use sparingly.

蓮葉 Lotus leaves. These leaves are dried and neatly stacked and tied. They must be thoroughly soaked, washed and scalded.

蓮蓉 Lotus nut paste. Made from lotus seeds, sugar, oil and water. Available in 16-oz. can. It is a smooth and delicate filling for buns, cookies and cakes.

綠豆芽 Mung bean sprouts. These sprouts are called green bean sprouts in Chinese. Plump, short rooted white sprouts are best. Gourmet cooks like to pluck off the roots (optional). Sprouts should be well rinsed and picked over. Discard green bean hulls and tired, yellow-looking sprouts. Adds a fresh crisp taste to food.

Mustard. Ready-made extra-hot Chinese-style mustard
芥辣
is available in spice jars at the supermarkets.

Oil. Peanut oil is the first choice. Other quality
油
vegetable oils may be used.

Oyster sauce. Its ingredients are oyster extracts,
蠔油
water, salt, starch, acetic acid, sodium benzoate
and caramel. Store in refrigerator after opening.

Parchment paper. Baking parchment papers are occa-
紙
sionally found in supermarkets. Most cake and
pastry supply shops have them in stock.

Potato starch. Available at delicatessens and
薯粉
natural food stores.

Pot sticker wrappers. Ready-made pot sticker skins
鍋貼皮
are available at the noodle factories and
Oriental shops. These wrappers are much thicker than the familiar won ton skins. Freeze or
refrigerate well-wrapped skins.

Plum sauce. A sauce made from sugar, plum plup,
vinegar, salt, ginger, chili and garlic. It
is available in 1-lb. cans. 蘇梅醬

Quail eggs. Peeled hard-cooked quail eggs are canned
鵪鶉蛋
in water. An ingredient present in many gourmet
dishes.

Red bean curd (nam yu). The smallest size is a 5-1/2
ounce can, containing 1 block fermented bean curd
南乳
and some sauce. It is labeled as "bean cake" or
"wet bean curd" which can be confused with the
canned beige-colored bean curd (fu yu). After
opening, store bean curd and its sauce in closed
jar in refrigerator.

Red bean paste. A ready-to-use paste, made from red
豆沙
beans, sugar and water. Available in 18-oz.
cans.

Rice noodles. See fun.

Salted duck eggs. Fresh duck eggs preserved with a
coat of salty ashes. The yolk is solid and red.
If hard-boiled, the yolk displays a few drops
鹹蛋
of oil. Salted eggs can be preserved as follows:
Dissolve coarse kosher salt, about 1 tablespoon
per egg, in boiling water; cool completely. Then
place eggs in a glass jar and pour salt water
over eggs to cover. Keep jar in a cool place.
The eggs will be ready in about one month.

Sesame oil. This is Oriental sesame oil, made from 蘇油 toasted sesame seeds. Widely available at the supermarkets. It adds aroma to food.

Shake-on dry lemon juice. This is a domestic product 檸檬粉 available at delicatessens, gourmet shops and some department stores.

Sherry. Any kind of sherry or Chinese wine may be 酒 used. Cream sherry adds a touch of sweetness to shrimp and beef, thereby eliminating the addition of sugar.

Soy sauces. Soy sauces are classified as thin (or 豉油 light) soy and dark (or black) soy. Thin soy is made from yellow beans, flour, salt and water; dark soy has molasses added. Thin soy is preferred for table condiment and soups; dark soy adds a deeper color to food.

Spring roll skins. Two types of spring roll skins 春捲皮 are available: the regular won ton skin type & the paper-thin type which looks similar to slightly wrinkled tissue paper. The latter is very fragile, but crispier in taste. Available in 1-lb. packs at noodle factories, Oriental markets and in the refrigerator or freezer section of most supermarkets. Freeze or re-frigerate well-wrapped skins.

Star anise. Its Chinese name means "eight corners". 八角 It has a very strong flavor. Break off individual pods. Two to four pods are usually sufficient.

Subgum sauce. Made from yellow beans, flour, sugar, 什錦醬 vinegar, salt and food color. Available in 1-lb. cans.

Sweet and sour sauce. Ready-to-use sweet and sour 甜酸醬 sauce is available in bottles. It can be used as dip or sauce. Available at all Oriental shops.

Sweet and sour duck sauce. A ready-to-use sweet and 甜酸鴨醬 sour sauce available at all Oriental markets. It can be used as a dip for deep-fried dumplings, roasted meat or fried poultry.

Sweet bean sauce. It's made from soy beans, flour, 甜麵醬 sugar, spices and bean sauce. It is not very sweet, but actually somewhat salty.

Sweet rice. See glutinous rice.

Sweet rice flour. See glutinous rice flour.

花椒 Szechwan peppercorns. Brown peppercorns available in small plastic bags. It is also called anise pepper. Widely used in northern Chinese cooking.

芋粉 Taro powder. An instant powder made from taro roots. This is not a fine powder; its texture is very similar to instant potato flakes. Available in 8-oz. packages.

炸蝦粉 Tempura batter mix. The ingredients are wheat flour, rice flour, cornstarch, baking powder and powdered egg. Widely available at the supermarkets.

齋鮑魚 Vegetarian abalone. Vegetarian abalone is really fried gluten with salt, sugar and soy sauce added. Most frequently labeled as *chai pow yu*. Available in 10-oz. cans.

粉絲 Vermicelli (also called bean threads). Made from mung bean starch. It is an ingredient added to many vegetarian or meat dishes. Deep-fried vermicelli are tossed in fresh salads.

War mein. A wider (about 5/16") flat noodle often used to make noodle soup. 窩麵

荸薺粉 Water chestnut powder. A fine powder used as thickener and batter. It gives a crisp light coating to deep-fried foods.

荸薺 Water chestnuts. Fresh or canned water chestnuts can be used in all the recipes. However, fresh water chestnuts are much better. Fresh water chestnuts are crunchy and sweet, similar to the fresh apples in September. Peel off the covering, rinse well, then eat them raw for snacks.

澄麵粉 Wheat starch. Available in 1-lb. packages. Sift upon opening a new package.

粘米粉 White rice flour. Natural food stores carry a large supply of rice flour and it is labeled as "white rice flour". Imported rice flour is often labeled as "rice flour". It is not to be confused with the "sweet rice flour" which is a glutinous flour. Sift imported rice flour with the finest meshed sifter. Imported rice flour and domestic product differ in dryness and texture. It may be necessary to adjust the amount of liquid to be used.

Won ton skins. Round skins are available in Oriental markets and noodle factories. Square skins are

雲
吞
皮
available at most supermarkets as well as Oriental markets. Freeze or refrigerate well-wrapped skins. If round won ton skins are not available, cut the square skins with scissors or a doughnut cutter. Doughnut cutter size is perfect for hors d'oeuvres. Deep-fry the leftover corners, crumble, and add to fresh salad. Or, sprinkle cinnamon-sugar over deep-fried won ton skins and serve for snacks. For homemade *won ton skins, spring roll skins* or *noodles*: Mix together 2 cups all-purpose flour, 2 large eggs (beaten), 1/4 teaspoon salt and approximately 3 tablespoons water; knead into a smooth non-sticky dough. Cover with a damp-ened towel and let rest for 20 minutes. Roll out the dough, on lightly floured surface, to desired thinness (even paper-thin thickness for that deep-fried crispness); cut into desired size and shape. Spread on counter to dry briefly until firm. Do not overdry; the dough will curl and crack. Lightly sprinkle flour over noodles or skins, then wrap for storage.

子
薑
Young spring ginger root. Tender young ginger roots which look white and pink in color. Available during spring-summer season. Excellent for making ginger beef.

TEA

(cha)

At a *dim sum* luncheon, tea is served first and as soon as everyone is seated. To the Chinese, tea is much more than just a beverage. Hot tea is served to guests upon arrival as a symbol of cordial reception. The host or hostess hands the tea to the guest with both hands holding the cup or saucer. Handing over a cup of tea with only one hand is regarded as discourteous. This custom is also observed by the recipient. Instead of having an alcoholic toast to celebrate the new year, Chinese offer tea and candied fruits as they say *gung hur sun hay!**

Tea is served ceremoniously at the time of marriage. The bride personally serves her parents, in-laws and even close relatives as a way of expressing respect. In return, they present her with jewelry or a small red envelope with a small amount of money in it as a way of expressing appreciation and wishing her happiness. Tea is formally served to the bride to welcome, accept and honor her by her new family.

Sugar, milk and lemon are not served with tea if it is served Chinese style. Flower teas, such as chrysanthemum, are exceptions; a pinch of sugar is often added. Black tea, which is called red tea in Chinese, is made by process of fermentation of the leaves while green tea is made by steaming the fresh leaves, then drying them. Curing techniques vary considerably. Tea, as we all know, is a stimulant because it contains caffeine. Its bitterness comes from the tannic acid.

There are numerous blends and varieties of tea. A few of the popular Chinese names are: *Ooloong*, a semi-fermented tea most widely served at home; *Lychee*, a favorite, sweet scented tea with the aroma of lychee fruit; *Po Nay*, a stronger black tea preferred by many *dim sum* diners; *Jasmine*, an ever popular fermented tea with enchanting fragrance of jasmine blossoms; *Tit Koon Yum* (iron goddess of mercy), a black tea well known and much praised among the Chinese; *Chrysanthemum*, that touch of sweetness gives this tea a clean and pure taste to sooth the lungs and throat; *Loong Jen* (dragon's well), rated as the finest green

* This expression actually means "wishing happy new year" in Chinese. The well-known phrase "gung hay fat choy" means "wishing prosperity".

13

tea, delicate and fragrant; *Ngun Jum* (silver needles), a mild delicate green tea; *So Mei* (eyebrows of longevity) and *Sui Sen* (water nymph) are two more green teas with natural scented fragrance. For the tea explorer, there are *Ching Yin* (clear distance), *Loong So* (dragon's beard), *Mo Yee, Wun Mo* (cloud mist), *Tit Lo Han* and a great many others. Perception of the fragrance and taste of any tea varies, needless to say, from individual to individual. One person may describe a particular blend as delicate and refreshing, another as slightly bitter.

The steeping time and the amount of tea leaves in proportion to the amount of water will depend on the kind of tea and one's personal taste. Some of us prefer the flavor and taste of the second or third pot, and some would never use the same leaves more than once. The type of tea plays an important role in this preference. There are probably as many methods of brewing tea as there are tea-drinkers. General directions are given below:

1 tablespoon tea leaves
4 cups vigorously boiling water

Start with clean utensils and fresh water. Rinse a round porcelain (or earthenware) teapot with boiling water. Drop tea leaves into the teapot and pour vigorously boiling water over leaves. Cover and let steep 3 to 5 minutes, according to "your cup of tea".

Saltish Dim Sum

FOUR-COLORED SHIU MAI, page 28

POT STICKER TRIANGLES, page 41

FUN GOR TORTELLINI, page 19

VEGETARIAN SPRING ROLLS, page 50

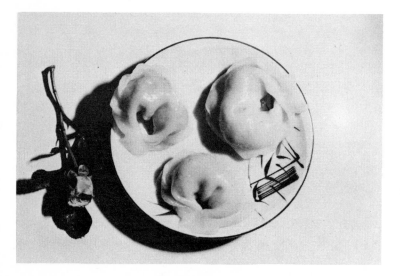

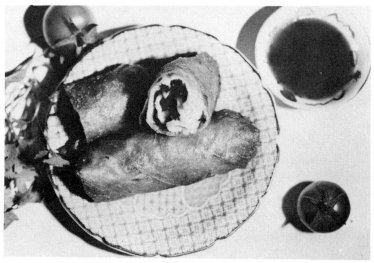

FUN GOR DOUGH 粉裹皮

1 cup cake flour
1/4 teaspoon salt
1/2 cup boiling water
1/2 teaspoon lard or shortening
cake flour for dusting

Measure flour and salt into a small mixing bowl.
Quickly pour boiling water into flour while stirring
to get a partially cooked dough. Add lard and knead
until smooth, adding more hot water or flour as
needed to make a workable dough. Keep covered. Let
rest for a few minutes before shaping.

TO MAKE FUN GOR AND ALL CRESCENT SHAPED PASTRIES

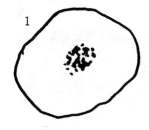

1. Fill rolled dough.
2. Fold in half and seal edges.
3. Crimp edges (optional) by holding crescent between thumb and fingers of one hand, with rounded edge
    up. Using sides of thumb and forefinger of other hand, pinch dough along edge of crescent, fluting
    it as you would pie crust.

粉 裹

1 recipe FUN GOR DOUGH, page 17
1 recipe BASIC PORK & SHRIMP FILLING, page 82
dip of choice

Prepare dough and filling as directed in recipes.

Lightly dust rolling pin and hands with flour.
Shape dough evenly into two 10" long rolls. Cut
rolls into 20 1-inch pieces.(It is better to break
off one piece of dough at a time. Dough will stay
moist and warm longer.) Roll each piece of dough
into a 3-inch circle. Place 2 teaspoons filling
in the center. Fold half of the circle over filling to form a half moon. Tightly seal and crimp
edges. Arrange *fun gor*, without touching, in a
single layer on well-greased steaming tray. Steam
over boiling water 15 to 18 minutes or until pork
is cooked. Serve hot.

Cooked, cooled and well-wrapped *fun gor* can be
refrigerated for 2 to 3 days. Reheat by steaming.

FUN GOR TORTELLINI
makes 20-24

乾蒸餃

1 recipe HAR GOW DOUGH, page 21
1 recipe PORK & CABBAGE FILLING, page 85
chili oil, mustard, soy sauce or mix any or all
of these in desired proportions for dip

Prepare dough and filling as directed. Lightly
dust rolling pin and hands with flour. Shape
dough evenly into two 10" long rolls. Cut rolls
into 20 1-inch pieces (or break off a little
piece at a time). Roll a piece of dough into a
3-inch circle. Place 2 teaspoons filling in the
center. Fold half of the circle over filling to
form a crescent (a narrower long-looking crescent
is best). Pinch edges to seal. Crimp sealed
edges by holding crescent between thumb and
fingers of one hand, with rounded edge up. Using
sides of thumb and forefinger of other hand,
pinch dough along edge of crescent, fluting it as
you would pie crust. Then, grasp the pastry with
thumbs and forefingers on each side, bend left
and right corners toward and beyond the uncrimped
side to overlap, making an X. Pinch crossing to
keep it in place. The resulting dumplings look
similar to the tortellini. Proceed similarly

until all the dumplings are made. Arrange dumplings,
without touching, in a single layer on well-greased
steaming trays. Steam until done, about 15 minutes.
Serve hot.

For advance preparation, refrigerate well-wrapped
cooked dumplings. Steam until hot, then serve.

1  2   3

1. Fill rolled
   dough.

2. Fold in
   half and
   seal.

3. Crimp the
   edges.

4   5

4. Bend corners toward
   uncrimped side.

5. Pinch crossing to
   keep it in place.

素食粉裹

1 recipe HAR GOW DOUGH, page 21

1 recipe VEGETARIAN FILLING, page 85

hot mustard, chili oil, soy sauce or sauce of
choice for dip

Prepare filling and dough as directed. Divide dough
into 20 pieces or break off one piece at a time.
Roll out a piece of dough into a 4-inch circle. Dot
the center with 2 teaspoons filling. Fold circle in
half over filling to form a half moon. Pinch and
seal the left and right edges near corners, leaving
half of the edges open in the middle to form a "canoe".
Holding both sealed corners, gently push upward toward
the center to form a "star". Seal remaining edges.
Repeat until all dumplings are made. Place dumplings
on greased steaming trays to steam until cooked, 15
to 18 minutes. Serve hot with dip.

Well-wrapped dumplings may be refrigerated for 2 to
3 days. Reheat by steaming.

TO MAKE "STAR" SHAPED VEGETARIAN FUN GOR

1. Fill rolled dough.

2. Fold in half and seal left and right sides,
    leaving middle open.

3. Holding both sealed corners, push upward
    toward center to form a "star".

4. Seal remaining edges.

HAR GOW DOUGH　　蝦 餃 皮

2　tablespoons potato starch
1　cup wheat starch
1/4　teaspoon salt
10　tablespoons boiling water
1　teaspoon lard or shortening
wheat starch for dusting

Measure both starches and salt into a small mixing bowl. Quickly pour boiling water into starches while stirring to get a partially cooked dough. Add lard and knead until smooth, adding more hot water or wheat starch as needed to make a workable dough. Cover and let rest for a few minutes before shaping.

HAR GOW DOUGH and FUN GOR DOUGH are interchangeable. HAR GOW DOUGH is nearly translucent, allowing the filling to "show". But if wheat starch and potato starch are not readily available, FUN GOR DOUGH is an excellent substitute.

TO MAKE HAR GOW SHAPED DUMPLINGS

1

2

3

1. Makes pleats on one side of rolled dough and fill.

2. Bring edges together and seal.

3. A finished *har gow* shaped dumpling.

1 recipe HAR GOW DOUGH, page 21

dip of choice

Filling: mix together

- 3/4 lb. raw medium prawns, shelled, deveined and diced
- 3/4 cup minced bamboo shoots
- 1/4 teaspoon minced fresh ginger (or ginger powder)
- 1 tablespoon minced fresh coriander or minced green onion
- 1/2 teaspoon salt
- 2 tablespoons cornstarch
- 1/8 teaspoon white pepper
- 1 teaspoon cream sherry
- 1 teaspoon *each* sesame oil and cooking oil
- 1/2 tablespoon *each* dark soy sauce and oyster sauce

Prepare dough as directed. Lightly dust rolling pin and hands with flour. Shape dough into two 11" long rolls. Cut rolls into 22 1-inch pieces (it is better to break off a piece at a time; dough will stay warm and moist longer). Roll each piece into a 3" circle. Fold 3 to 5 pleats on the half circle near you, resembling a jacket hood with a ruffled top. Pinch

along the edge to keep the pleats in place. Stuff the cavity with 2 to 3 teaspoons of filling. Bring edge of the far side over to meet the edge of the pleated side. Pinch and seal tightly. Place *har gow*, seam side up and without touching, in a single layer on well greased steaming trays (a heatproof plate may be used, but the steaming tray is better). Keep covered while working with remaining dough. Steam over boiling water 15 to 18 minutes. Serve hot.

Cooled dumplings may be refrigerated for 2 to 3 days in sealed containers. Reheat by steaming.

FLOWERET SHIU MAI
makes 20-24

花形燒賣

1 recipe HAR GOW DOUGH, page 21
1 recipe TURKEY FILLING or SPICY TURKEY FILLING,
   page 84
dip of choice

Prepare dough and filling as directed. Lightly dust
rolling pin and hands with flour. Shape dough evenly
into two 10" long rolls. Cut rolls into 20 1-inch
pieces (or break off a piece at a time). Roll out
a piece of dough into a 3-inch circle. Place 2 teaspoons filling in the center and gather edges upward
toward the center. Gently squeeze sack with the arc
between thumb and index finger to get an open sack
with a narrower neck, pressing filling down at the
same time. The sack should have 1/8" unfilled edges.
Spread the unfilled edges outward and pinch to form
flower petals. Repeat until all the dumplings are
made. Arrange dumplings, right side up and without
touching, in a single layer on well-greased steamer.
Steam until done, 15 to 18 minutes. Serve hot.

Cooked dumplings can be refrigerated for 2 to 3 days.
To reheat, steam until hot.

23

round won ton skins, see won ton skins, page 11
1 recipe BASIC PORK & SHRIMP FILLING, page 82
1 15-oz. can quail eggs, drained
mustard, chili oil or soy sauce for dip

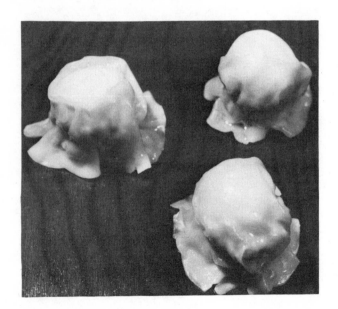

Prepare filling as directed. Place an egg and top
it with 1 heaping teaspoon filling (in this order)
in the center of a won ton skin. Gather edges upward toward center. Gently squeeze sack with the
arc between thumb and index finger to get an open
sack with a narrower neck, pressing filling down at
the same time. If needed, use a dab of water to
help keep the pleats in place. The sack should
have 1/8" unfilled edge. Repeat until filling is
all used. Arrange *shiu mai*, upside down and with
the unfilled edges spreading out, on greased steaming trays to steam until done, about 15 minutes.
Serve hot with dip.

Refrigerate well-wrapped dumplings. To reheat,
steam until hot.

A finished *shiu mai*

Place *shiu mai* upside
down on steaming tray

round won ton skins, see won ton skins, page 11

1　recipe BASIC PORK & SHRIMP FILLING, page 82
　　or GROUND PORK FILLING, page 82

dip of choice

red bell pepper bits, green peas, small bits of
salted duck egg yolk or diced Chinese pork sausage
for garnish

Prepare filling as directed. Work with one won ton
skin at a time, keeping the rest covered. Spread won
ton skin on kitchen counter and place a tablespoon
filling in the center of the wrapper. Moisten all
around the circular edges with a dab of water (only
if needed), then gather edges upward around the filling to form a pleated pouch with an open top. Gently
squeeze *shiu mai* with the arc between thumb and index
finger while turning it so wrapper will cling to the
meat mixture, at the same time pressing and leveling
the filling down with a small knife. Press a bit of
garnish on top of the filling. Repeat with remaining
filling. Arrange *shiu mai* in a single layer, garnished
side up and without touching, on greased steaming tray.
Steam over boiling water 18 to 20 minutes. Serve hot
with or without dip.

Cooked *shiu mai* can be refrigerated for 2 to 3 days
or frozen. Reheat by steaming.

RICE SHIU MAI
makes 3 dozen　　糯米燒賣

round won ton skins, see won ton skins, page 11
marinated raw prawns, see SHRIMP ROLLS, page 49
Glutinous Rice Filling:

1	cup glutinous rice
3/4	cup boiling water
1/2	lb. bacon, crisp fried and finely crumbled
1/4	lb. shelled cooked shrimp, minced
2	teaspoons soy sauce
1-1/2	tablespoons oyster sauce
1/4	teaspoon Chinese 5-spice
1	green onion, minced
1/4	teaspoon salt
1	teaspoon sesame oil

Wash rice and soak several hours. Drain, but do not
dry. Grease a 2-quart heavy-bottomed saucepan having
a tight lid. Pour rice into pan. Add boiling water
to rice and cook over high heat, stirring constantly
while rice is boiling. When rice has absorbed most of
the water, make a well in the center; cover lid and
reduce heat to medium-low for 5 to 6 minutes. Then,
reduce heat to simmer and let stand for at least 15
more minutes. Uncover, fluff up the grains and spoon
all the rice, except bottom crust (see note below),
into a mixing bowl. Add remaining filling ingredients
and mix well. Use for stuffing (great for poultry) or
serve as a rice dish.

Prepare prawns as directed. Work with one won ton
skin at a time, keeping the rest covered. Spread won
ton skin on kitchen counter and place a tablespoon
filling in the center of the wrapper. Moisten all
around the circular edges with water (if needed), then
gather edges upward around the filling to form a
pleated pouch with an open top, moistening the pleats
with water to keep them in place. Firmly press filling down and garnish with a half shrimp. Repeat with
remaining filling. Arrange *rice shiu mai* in a single
layer, garnished side up and without touching, on
greased steaming trays. Steam over boiling water until
won ton skin is cooked through and soft, about 10
minutes. Serve hot. Soy sauce or oyster sauce can be
served as accompaniment.

Note. Add a small amount of water to rice crust
and simmer until soft. Add a pinch of salt,
seasoning and leftover meat or vegetables. It
makes a wholesome snack.

FANCY FANS
makes about 2 dozen

扇 餃

round won ton skins, see won ton skins, page 11

1 recipe SPICY SHRIMP FILLING, page 86
    or TURKEY FILLING, page 84

sauce of choice for dip

Prepare filling as directed. Spread won ton skins
on counter and place 2 to 3 teaspoons filling in
the center of each wrapper. Working with one skin
at a time, fold circle in half to form a crescent.
Pinch edges to seal. Crease the curved edge, forming
pleats. Pinch pleats to keep them in place, using
a dab of water if needed. Repeat with remaining
filled skins. Arrange dumplings in a single layer,
without touching, on greased steaming trays. Steam
over boiling water for 15 minutes or until cooked.
Serve *immediately*.

For advance preparation, refrigerate or freeze well-
wrapped cooked dumplings. Reheat by steaming.

四喜燒賣

1 recipe HAR GOW DOUGH, page 21
1 recipe BASIC PORK & SHRIMP FILLING, page 82
chili sauce, hot mustard or soy sauce for dip

Prepare filling and dough as directed. Lightly dust
rolling pin and hands with flour. Shape dough evenly
into two 10" long rolls. Cut rolls into 20 1-inch
pieces (or break off a small piece of dough at a
time). Roll out a piece of dough into a 3-inch
circle. Place 2 teaspoons filling in the center.
Fold half of the circle over filling to form a
crescent. Do not seal edges. Using thumb and forefinger, grasp each side of curved part 1/4 of the

distance up from base of crescent. Push toward the
center and pinch to meet at a point, allowing all 4
corners to fall open. Hold *shiu mai* between the thumb
and the index finger and gently squeeze so the *shiu
mai* will have a taller cylinderical appearance. Pinch
sides together as indicated in step 5. Garnish the
open corners with different colored ingredients (a bit
of shrimp, mushroom, water chestnut and green onion).
Proceed similarly with remaining dough and cover the
dumplings with a dampened cloth. Arrange dumplings,
without touching, on greased steaming tray. Steam
over boiling water until done, about 15 minutes. Serve
hot with or without dip.

Well-wrapped dumplings may be refrigerated for 2 to
3 days. Reheat by steaming.

1

1. Fill rolled
   dough.

2. Grasp at points
   A and B.

3. and 4. Push toward center
   to meet at a point,
   but allowing corners
   to fall open.

5

5. Pinch sides
   together
   indicated by
   arrows.

6. Garnish
   open
   corners.

CRYSTAL SHIU MAI
makes 20-24　　水晶餃

1 recipe HAR GOW DOUGH, page 21
1 recipe BASIC PORK & SHRIMP FILLING, page 82
mustard, chili oil or soy sauce for dip

Prepare dough and filling as directed. Divide dough
into 20-24 pieces. Roll out a piece of dough into a
3-inch circle. Dot the center with 2 to 3 teaspoons
filling. Fold circle in half and pinch mid-point to
stick together (use a dab of water if needed). Bring
opposite sides closer together and pinch left and
right corners to stick. Repeat with remaining filling.
Arrange the dumplings in a single layer, without touching, on greased steaming tray. Steam over boiling
water until done, about 15 minutes. Serve hot with or
without dip. Well-wrapped cooked dumplings may be
refrigerated for 2 to 3 days. Reheat by steaming.

side 1

side 1

3

4

side 2

side 2

1

side 2   side 1

2

1. Fill rolled
dough.

2. Fold in half. Pinch
midpoint to stick
together.
HORIZONTAL POSITION

3. Top view of
No. 2 placed
in a
VERTICAL POSITION

4. Bring side 1
and side 2
closer together.
Pinch corners to
stick together.

29

BOILED DUMPLINGS WITH DIP 水餃
makes 15

1 recipe filling of choice, see recipes

soy sauce, mustard, chili oil or other sauces
for dip

Wrapper:

   1-1/2 cups all-purpose flour

      pinch of salt

   1 teaspoon oil

   6 to 7 tablespoons cold water

      additional flour for dusting

Prepare filling as directed. Stir flour, oil and
salt in a small mixing bowl. Gradually add water
while stirring to form a dough. Knead until smooth.
Divide dough into 15 equal pieces. Make dumplings
into crescents or *har gow* shaped dumplings. Drop
dumplings into rapidly boiling water. Cook, uncovered and stirring often, until done, about four
minutes. Drain and serve with dip. See FUN GOR
DOUGH or HAR GOW DOUGH recipe for dumpling making
directions.

叉燒角 SAVORY FLAKY TRIANGLES
makes 16

1 recipe FLAKY BAKING PASTRY DOUGH, page 37

1 recipe CHAR SHIU FILLING, page 81
   or STIR-FRIED PORK FILLING, page 83
   or Bacon & Chicken Filling, page 36

Mix:

   1 egg yolk

   2 teaspoons water

Prepare dough and filling as directed.. Take a square
of dough; roll it out into a 4"x4" square. Dot the
center with 1 tablespoon filling. Fold square in half
diagonally to form a triangle. Seal edges tightly by
pressing with tines of a fork. Place on greased baking sheet. Prick top and brush with yolk mixture.
Repeat process. Bake in preheated 350° F. oven until
lightly golden, 20 to 25 minutes.

Baked flaky pastries freeze well. Reheat in slow oven.

VARIATION: Choose a curried filling and make BAKED
CURRIED TURNOVERS.

STEAMED BUN DOUGH　　蒸飽皮

You may choose Steamed Bun Dough #1 or Steamed Bun Dough #2. Steamed Bun Dough #2 has a sweeter and firmer texture, is easier to handle, and the *bao* will hold its shape better.

Steamed Bun Dough #1:

2-3/4　teaspoons or 1 packet active dry yeast
1　cup plus 3 tablespoons warm water ($105°$ to $115°$ F.)
3/4　teaspoon salt
6　tablespoons sugar
2　tablespoons melted shortening
4　cups all-purpose flour
　all-purpose flour for dusting

Steamed Bun Dough #2:

2-3/4　teaspoons or 1 packet active dry yeast
1　cup warm water
3/4　teaspoon salt
1/2　cup sugar
1　tablespoon melted shortening
1-1/2　cups white rice flour
2-1/2　cups all-purpose flour
　all-purpose flour for dusting

Add a tablespoon of the measured sugar to the dry yeast; stir. Add water to yeast mixture; blend. When the yeast and sugar have dissolved completely, add shortening. Combine flour, salt and remaining sugar in a large bowl and stir a few times to mix. Gradually pour yeast mixture into flour mixture while stirring to form a dough. Let rest 5 minutes. Turn out onto lightly floured surface. Knead until smooth and elastic. Place dough in a greased bowl, cover with towel and let rise in warm place until dough is at least doubled (you should get one large mixing bowl full), 1-1/2 hours to 2 hours. Punch

down, cover and let rest a few minutes before shaping.

NOTE. When the kitchen is warm, around $80°$ F. and with the air conditioning turned off, it is the best place and time to make *bao*. The cook may "roast" for a few hours, but will smile at the creations.

CRESCENT-SHAPED STEAMED BUNS

makes 20 buns

1 recipe STEAMED BUN DOUGH, page 31
20 2-1/2"x2" parchment papers
oil

Prepare dough as directed in recipe. Dust hands
with flour. Shape dough evenly into two 10" long
rolls. Cut rolls into 20 1-inch pieces. Flatten
each piece into a 3" to 3-1/2" circle. Brush top
with oil. Fold in half with the oiled sides together and lightly press the edges together so
that the edges are thinner and somewhat sealed.
Set bun on a parchment paper, then put into steamer,
2" apart. Cover with cloth and let rise until
almost doubled in bulk, 10 to 20 minutes. Set
over boiling water and steam until done, about 10
minutes. Serve with CRISPY DUCK or CRISP SOY
SAUCE SQUABS/GAME HENS.

Steamed buns freeze well. Steam thawed or unthawed
buns until hot, then serve.

VARIATION: Make FAN-SHAPED STEAMED BUNS. Flatten
each piece of dough to a 3-1/2" circle. Fold in
half and press edges. With a chopstick, pull dough

back at points A and B to resemble figure 2. Cover;
let rise and steam as directed above.

FAN-SHAPED STEAMED BUNS

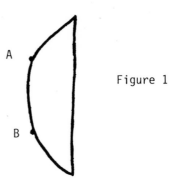

Figure 1

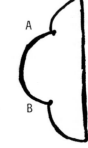

Figure 2

Pull dough back at
points A and B.

CHAR SHIU BAO
makes 20 steamed buns

叉 燒 飽

20 3-inch circular parchment papers
 1 recipe STEAMED BUN DOUGH, page 31
 1 recipe CHAR SHIU FILLING, page 81

Prepare dough and filling as directed. Flour hands.
Shape dough evenly into two 10" long rolls. Cut
rolls into 20 1-inch pieces. Stretch and shape
each piece into a 4-inch circle. Fill with one
tablespoon meat mixture. Bring round edges together
to enclose filling, pleating it as you go along.
Then, twist the pleated edges at the top to insure
a secure seal. Set bun on a piece of paper with
the seam side up. (For beginners, simply roll the
bun into a ball and place it on paper with the seam
side down.) Proceed similarly with remaining dough.
Arrange buns 2" apart on bamboo steamer, steaming
tray, or 10" cake racks. Cover with cloth and let
rise until the *dough* is almost doubled in bulk, 10
to 20 minutes. Steam above boiling water over high
heat for 10 to 12 minutes. Serve hot or cold.

1   recipe STEAMED BUN DOUGH, page 31
2   7"x7" parchment papers
Mix:

    1   lb. bacon, crisp fried, finely crumbled
        and crushed

   1/2   cup minced green onion

Prepare dough as directed, then cut it in halves.
Roll out one piece of the dough into a rectangle of
1/4" thickness. Sprinkle one-twelfth filling in the
center third of the rectangle. Fold left third over
filling to cover. Sprinkle 1/12 filling on top and
fold right side over filling. Repeat this process
twice. The result is a triple-folded dough, about
6" square by 1-1/2" thick. Place on paper and set
on steaming tray or 10" cake rack (bamboo steamer is
best). Cover with cloth to let rise. Now, roll and
fill the other half of dough. Also cover to let rise
for about 30 minutes. Steam over boiling water (set
on high heat) until done, about 15 minutes. Turn
out, cool, then cut with a sharp knife.

Cooked cooled bread can be frozen. Steam before
serving.

BAKED CHAR SHIU BAO
makes 16 buns

焗餐飽

Dough:

    1   packet active dry yeast

    1   cup warm water (105^0 to 115^0 F.)

 1/4 teaspoon salt

 1/3 cup sugar

    2   large eggs

    4   to 4-1/4 cups all-purpose flour

       all-purpose flour for dusting

1   recipe CHAR SHIU FILLING, page 81
   or CHAR SHIU WITH ONION FILLING, page 81

Dissolve yeast in warm water. Beat eggs with sugar and salt. Gradually add dissolved yeast and half the flour, beating until smooth. By hand, stir in the remaining flour. Let rest for 5 minutes. Turn out onto lightly floured surface; knead until elastic and smooth. Place dough in a greased bowl, cover with towel and let rise in warm place until dough is at least doubled, 1-1/2 hours to 2 hours. Punch down, cover and let rest a few minutes before shaping.

Dust hands with flour. Shape dough evenly into two 8" long rolls. Cut rolls into 16 1-inch pieces. Stretch a piece of dough into a 4" circle and dot the center with 2 tablespoons filling. Gather edges to enclose filling, then roll into a ball. Place bun in well-greased muffin tin. Repeat until all 16 buns are made. Cover with cloth and let rise until the *dough* is almost doubled in bulk, about 30 minutes. Bake in a preheated 350^0 F. oven until golden, about 20 minutes. Remove buns from muffin pans. Serve hot or cold.

Baked char shiu bao can be served for breakfast, lunch, family dinner, company dinner or carry them along to a picnic.

五香小飽

2   cans refrigerated extra-light buttermilk biscuit
    dough
Bacon and Chicken Filling:
        3   strips bacon, crisp-fried and crumbled
1-1/2   to 2 tablespoons oil
        1   green onion, minced
        1   tablespoon oyster sauce
        1   whole large chicken breast, skinned, boned,
            minced and marinated in:
                1   tablespoon cornstarch
              1/4   teaspoon salt
              1/2   teaspoon Chinese 5-spice
                1   tablespoon dark soy sauce
        Thickener: blend
                2   teaspoons cornstarch
              1/4   cup water

Stir-fry chicken in 1-1/2 to 2 tablespoons hot oil
until cooked. Add cornstarch mixture and stir until
thickened. Add onion, bacon and oyster sauce; mix
well.

Separate biscuit dough into 20 pieces. Stretch a
piece of dough into a 3" circle and dot the center
with 2 teaspoons filling. Bring edges together to
enclose filling. Twist the gathered edges to insure
a secure seal and roll into a ball. Place in greased
mini muffin pan. Proceed similarly until done. Bake
in a 350° F. oven until golden, about 15 minutes.

Wrap and refrigerate leftover biscuits. Reheat in
slow oven until warm, then serve.

These mini biscuits can be served for breakfast,
lunch, dinner or hors d'oeuvres. Take them along
on a picnic, too.

Dough A:

   2   cups all-purpose flour

1/4   cup vegetable shortening

   2   teaspoons sugar

   2   pinches of salt

6-2/3   to 7 tablespoons ice cold water

Dough B:

   1   cup all-purpose flour

1/4   cup lard

2-1/2   teaspoons ice cold water

To make dough A: Measure flour, shortening, sugar and salt into mixing bowl. Blend with pastry blender until fine. Gradually add water and knead several times to form somewhat a smooth dough. *DO NOT OVER-WORK DOUGH.*

Repeat the above procedure with dough B. Dough B should be somewhat dry and crumbly.

Divide each dough into 16 equal pieces. Flatten a piece of dough A. Place a piece of dough B in the center and wrap around with dough A to form a ball. Roll out on smooth surface to a 1/4" thick rectangle. Then, starting with a short side, roll up into a stick. Turn stick so that one end points toward you, and roll out into a rectangle of approximately 1-1/2" by 6". Starting with a narrow end, fold up to get a 4-layered square. Keep covered. Repeat until all the squares are made. Now, the flaky pastry dough is ready to be rolled out into circles for filling.

This may sound time consuming, but the actual work goes quite fast. The resulting pastry is worth the effort.

The best way to roll out the dough is to: Roll out 2 or 3 times, turn dough over; roll out 2 or 3 times and turn dough over; etc. The dough rolls out much easier, resulting in flakier crust.

CHAR SHIU SO
makes 16 baked flaky buns

义烧酥

1 recipe FLAKY BAKING PASTRY DOUGH, page 37
1 recipe CHAR SHIU WITH ONION FILLING, page 81
white sesame seeds
Mix:

      1   egg yolk
      2   teaspoons water

Prepare filling and dough as directed. Take a square
of dough and roll it out into a 4" circle. Place 1
tablespoon filling in the center. Gather edges and
pleat all the way around, twisting gathered edges at
the top to enclose completely. Brush top and sides
with yolk mixture and sprinkle sesame seeds over
bun. Place on greased baking sheet. Repeat until
all buns are made. Bake at 350° F. until golden, 25
to 30 minutes. Serve warm or cold.

Char shiu so is a scrumptious dim sum food. The
savory filling is indescribably delicious and the
flaky crust melts in the mouth! You guessed it--
it's my favorite!

LAYERED ONION PANCAKES 葱油薄餅
makes 10 pancakes

Dough:
    1-1/2   cups all-purpose flour
    1/2   teaspoon salt
    10   tablespoons boiling water
            all-purpose flour for dusting
Filling:
    1   small (4 oz.) sweet Spanish onion, finely
            chopped
    1   green onion, minced
oil for frying

Mix flour and salt in a small mixing bowl. Add boiling water; stir well. Knead into a dough, adding
more water if needed. Dough should be pliable, soft,
but not sticky. Cover and let rest for 10 minutes.

Heat 1 tablespoon oil until hot; add chopped onion
and stir-fry until golden brown. Mix in green
onion. Set aside.

Divide dough into 10 equal pieces. Lightly dust
rolling pin and smooth surface. Roll out a piece
of dough into a 4" circle. Sprinkle 1/10 of the
onion mixture on top; roll up into a stick. Turn
stick so that one end points toward you. Roll out

into a 5" by 1-1/4" rectangle. Fold up to get a
4-layered square. Roll out the square into a 4"
to 5" circle. Place on a waxed paper (for easier
handling and stacking). Cover with towel. Repeat
with remaining dough.

Heat and coat a skillet with a generous amount of
oil (adding more oil as needed), pan-fry pancakes
over medium-low heat until both sides are golden
brown. For a flakier pancake, swirl pan around on
burner occasionally to keep the pancake moving.
Serve hot.

Pancakes may be frozen. Wrap in aluminum foil,
reheat in slow oven until almost hot. Unwrap and
continue to heat until hot. Or, pop them in the
toaster!

VARIATION: Make CHINESE SAUSAGE PANCAKES. Steam
two links Chinese pork sausage for about 20 minutes,
then finely mince. Mix minced sausage with one green
onion, also finely minced. Use this for filling.
Delicious!

MANDARIN PANCAKES
makes 14 pancakes
薄餅

Mandarin Pancake Dough or Pot Sticker Dough:
    2   cups sifted all-purpose flour
    1/4 teaspoon salt
    3/4 cup boiling water
    1   tablespoon cold water
        all-purpose flour for dusting
oil or sesame oil for brushing

Measure flour and salt into mixing bowl. Gradually
add boiling water while stirring. Add cold water
and stir well to form a dough. Turn out onto lightly
floured surface; knead only until smooth. Cover
with dampened towel and let rest for 15 minutes.

Divide dough into 14 equal portions. Roll into balls.
Lightly flour rolling pin and board. Flatten a ball
to a 3" circle and thoroughly brush the top and edge
with oil. Flatten a second ball to a 3" circle and
place it over the oiled circle--sandwich style. Roll
out the "sandwich" into a 6" circle. Set aside on
a piece of waxed paper (for easier handling & stacking); cover with dampened towel. Proceed similarly
with remaining dough.

Over medium-low to medium heat, heat an ungreased but
well "seasoned" flat-bottomed pan until hot. Remove
a "sandwich" and put into pan. Wait for 20 seconds
or until it becomes non-stick, then turn over. Wait
for 20 seconds, then rotate "sandwich" quickly with
hand or chopsticks until small golden spots barely
become visible on the bottom. Turn over and rotate
as above to cook the other side in the same manner.
Do not permit pancakes to brown. Remove from pan,
separate "sandwich" into single pancakes and stack
on platter. Cover with towel until ready to serve.

Pancakes can be made in advance. Wrap pancakes well
in foil; refrigerate or freeze. Reheat by steaming
with foil wrapping on for about 10 minutes or until
soft.

Mandarin pancakes are usually served with MO SHU PORK
(see recipe) or Peking duck. For a delightful gastronomical treat, try these pancakes with our very
own CRISPY DUCK (see recipe).

三角鍋貼

round won ton skins or pot sticker wrappers
(available at Oriental markets)

one can chicken broth

cooking oil

Filling: mix together

   12 to 14 oz. skinless chicken meat (one large
      chicken breast), coarsely minced

  1/2 lb. pork (not too lean, not too fat),
      minced

    1 green onion, minced

    1 (or 2) thin slice ginger, *well* minced

  1/4 cup finely minced celery

    2 tablespoons cornstarch

    1 teaspoon salt

    4 teaspoons curry powder

    1 teaspoon *each* sesame oil and cooking oil

    1 egg

Fill a wrapper with 2 teaspoons filling. Fold half
of the circle over filling to form a half moon.
Seal corner on one side. Push the middle of the
open edge upward toward the center to form a triangle. Seal edges. Repeat until all filling is
used.

Heat skillet. Add one to two tablespoons oil (add
more oil as needed) and heat until hot. Brown pot
stickers on all sides (if possible) to get a nice
color. Remove excess oil from pan. Add enough
broth to just cover the bottom of the pan; cover
lid and simmer until done and the liquid has been
absorbed, but the pan and the pot stickers should
not be dry, about 5 minutes. Serve with or without
dip.

Cooked pot stickers can be refrigerated or frozen.
Wrap in foil and reheat in slow oven until hot or
reheat over medium-low heat in a lightly oiled
skillet with a very small amount of liquid similar
to the cooking method above.

1. Fill dough.
2. Fold in half & seal 1/3 of the edges on one side.
3. Bring middle of open edge upward toward center.
4. Seal all edges.

POT STICKERS
makes 30 to 36 　鍋貼

1 recipe Pot Sticker Dough, see MANDARIN PANCAKES
   on page 40
1 recipe TURKEY FILLING, page 84
   or BASIC PORK & SHRIMP FILLING, page 82
   or CURRIED BEEF FILLING, page 83
1 can clear chicken broth or beef broth
dip of choice

Prepare dough and filling as directed. Lightly dust
rolling pin and hands with flour. Shape dough into
2 equal long rolls. Cut rolls into 30-36 equal
pieces.(It is better to break off a piece at a time.
The dough stays warm and moist longer.) Roll out
a piece of dough into a 3" circle. Dot the center
with 2 teaspoons filling. Fold half of the circle
over filling to form a crescent. As you pinch to
seal the edges, make one or two small pleats near
each corner. Place on flat surface with the seam
side straight up and the round smooth side down;
gently press the pot sticker down to help it "sit
up straight" on the rounded edge. Repeat with
remaining dough.

Heat a large skillet. Add about 2 tablespoons oil
(add more as needed) and heat until hot. Brown pot

stickers in that same "sitting straight up" position.
Turn and brown the sides to get a nice color (this
is optional). Remove any excess oil. Add enough
broth to barely cover the bottom of the pan; cover
and simmer until the liquid has been absorbed, but
the pot stickers are not dry or burned. Serve with
or without dip.

Pot stickers can be refrigerated or frozen, cooked
or uncooked. Thaw uncooked pot stickers first, then
cook as directed above. To reheat cooked pot stickers: Wrap in foil and place in slow oven until soft
and hot or reheat over medium-low heat in a lightly
oiled skillet with a very small amount of liquid
similar to the cooking method above.

VARIATION: Make crescent-shaped pot stickers without the pleats. Place and cook pot stickers with
the seam side straight up as directed above.

POT STICKERS

鍋貼餅　　POT STICKER PATTY CAKES
makes 10

1 recipe Pot Sticker Dough, see MANDARIN PANCAKES
  on page 40
1 recipe CHAR SHIU WITH ONION FILLING, page 81
  or STIR-FRIED PORK FILLING, page 83
oil for cooking

Prepare dough and filling as directed. Divide dough
into 10 equal portions. Lightly dust hands with
flour. Pat and thin out a piece of dough into a
3-1/2" circle. Dot the center with a tablespoon
filling. Gather edges and pinch to completely enclose filling. With hands, gently flatten it to a
2-1/2" round. Set aside and cover with towel. Proceed with remaining dough.

Heat a large skillet until hot. Coat it with a
generous amount of oil. When hot, add patty cakes
and pan-fry both sides over medium heat until golden
brown and the dough is cooked through. Drain on
absorbent toweling. Serve plain or with dip.

These patty cakes can be refrigerated or frozen,
cooked or uncooked. To reheat cooked cakes, wrap
in foil and bake in a slow oven until soft. Thaw
uncooked cakes and cook as directed above.

PAN-FRIED PORK AND SHRIMP PATTIES 乾煎肉餅
makes 14 to 16 patties

Mix together and let stand for 30 minutes:

- 1/2 lb. raw medium prawns, shelled, deveined and diced
- 1/2 lb. ground pork
- 1 or 2 green onions, minced
- 1/8 teaspoon grated orange peel (or dried Chinese tangerine peel)
- 6 tablespoons minced bamboo shoots
- 1 or 2 slices fresh ginger, minced (or 1/4 teaspoon ground ginger)
- 1 egg
- 2 tablespoons cornstarch
- 1/2 teaspoon salt
- 1/8 teaspoon ground pepper
- 1 teaspoon sesame oil
- 1 tablespoon *each* oyster sauce & dark soy sauce

oil for frying

Heat, then coat a skillet with a generous amount of oil. Wait until the oil is hot. Spoon mixture into pan, using 2 tablespoons for each patty. Fry over medium-low heat for 1/2 minute, then turn over and flatten to form patties. Turn frequently and cook until done and golden, about 5 minutes. Serve hot or cold, plain or with dip of choice.

Patties freeze well. Reheat in slow oven until hot.

This mixture makes an excellent filling for *won ton*, *pot stickers*, *fun gor*, etc. It may be prepared one day in advance and kept in refrigerator.

Serve patties for lunch or dinner. Or, cut them into bite-sized pieces and serve as hors d'oeuvres. Also, try a pork and shrimp patty sandwich.

SHRIMP TOAST
an excellent hors d'oeuvre
蝦仁麵飽

8 slices white or wheat bread, crusts trimmed off
oil for deep-frying or pan-frying
Filling: mix

- 1/2 lb. raw medium prawns, shelled, deveined, minced
- 1/4 lb. pork, finely minced, preferably chopped with cleaver
- 1 green onion, minced
- 6 water chestnuts, finely minced
- 1 tablespoon cornstarch
- 1/2 teaspoon salt
- 1/8 teaspoon ground pepper
- 1/2 tablespoon light soy sauce
- 1 teaspoon cream sherry

Spread 1/8 of the filling over one side of each
slice of bread. Lower bread, meat side down, into
365° F. hot oil and fry until golden, 1 to 1-1/2
minutes. Turn over and fry the bread side until
delicately golden, 20 to 30 seconds. Drain on
absorbent papers. Cut into desired size and shape.
Serve plain or with duck sauce (a sweet and sour
sauce available in jars).

To pan-fry: Lightly coat a skillet with oil. Heat
until hot. Pan-fry toast over medium-low heat, meat
side down, for 2 to 2-1/2 minutes to a golden brown.
Turn over and slightly brown the other side. Cut
and serve. This is much lower in fat content, and
the toast is crisp and tasty.

Shrimp toast can be served as hors d'oeuvres, dim
sum, or picnic food. Refrigerate or freeze leftovers; reheat in oven until hot and crisp. If the
filling is not too thick, uncut toast can be reheated
in the toaster.

FRIED CURRIED BEEF WON TON

makes 4 dozen

炸雲呑

square won ton skins, see won ton skins, page 11

1 recipe CURRIED BEEF FILLING, page 83

oil for deep-frying

sauce of choice for dip, see SAUCES AND DIPS

Prepare filling as directed. To make conventional shaped won ton: Lay a won ton skin on counter with a corner pointing toward you. Place 1 teaspoon filling near the far corner. Fold this corner over the filling to cover, then roll over once toward you. Grasp filled skin with thumbs and forefingers on each side of filling (thumbs on top side of skin). Bend flaps away from you and filling toward you, making a 90° turn on each side by creasing skin near filling so flaps stay flat. Now lay the flaps over each other, making an X. Moisten crossing with a dab of water and pinch tightly. Proceed similarly until filling is all used. Freeze or refrigerate leftover skins.

To make triangular shaped won ton: Lay a square won ton skin on counter with a corner pointing toward you. Place 1 teaspoon filling near the far corner. Fold this corner over the filling to cover. Moisten

the areas on both sides of filling with a dab of water, then roll over once toward you. Pinch both sides of filling to insure a tight seal.

Deep-fry won ton, a few at a time, in hot oil until cooked through and golden, about 1-1/2 minutes. Serve plain or with dip. Cooked won ton can be frozen. Reheat in slow oven, thawed or unthawed, until hot and crisp. Do not burn. Leftover won ton can be used to make soup, see page 56.

VARIATION: Make DEEP-FRIED PORK & SHRIMP won ton with BASIC PORK & SHRIMP filling. Deep-fry longer until filling is cooked through. Serve with sweet & **sour s**auce.

TRIANGULAR SHAPED WON TON

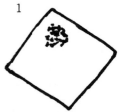

1. Fill dough.
2. Fold corner over filling. Moisten areas on both sides of filling, then roll over once. Pinch both sides of filling.

CONVENTIONAL SHAPED WON TON

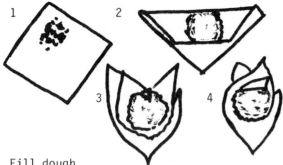

1. Fill dough.
2. Fold corner over filling and roll over once.
3. Bring side flaps away from you.
4. Lay flaps over each other. Moisten crossing and pinch to seal.

雲吞角 DEEP-FRIED WON TON CRESCENTS
makes 3 to 4 dozen

round won ton skins, see won ton skins, page 11
oil for deep-frying
1   recipe STIR-FRIED PORK FILLING, page 83
    or CHAR SHIU WITH ONION FILLING, page 81
dip of choice

Prepare filling as directed. Fill a piece of won ton skin with 2 teaspoons filling. Fold in half. Seal edges with a dab of water or beaten egg. Repeat with remaining filling. Deep-fry in hot oil (about 350° F.) until evenly golden. Drain on absorbent papers. Serve with or without dip.

These dumplings can be refrigerated for a few days or frozen for a longer period. Reheat in slow oven until hot and crisp. Do not burn.

SWEET AND SALTY CRESCENTS 甜鹹油角
makes 24

1 recipe BASIC SWEET DOUGH, page 93
1 recipe CHAR SHIU FILLING, page 81
   or Bacon & Chicken Filling, see 5-SPICED
   BISCUITS, page 36
oil for deep-frying

Prepare filling and dough as directed. Lightly
dust rolling pin and hands with flour. Shape
dough evenly into two 12" long rolls. Cut rolls
into 24 1-inch pieces. Roll dough, one piece at
a time, into a 2-1/2" to 3" circle. Place 2 teaspoons filling in the center. Fold circle in half
over filling to form a half moon. Tightly seal
and crimp edges (see FUN GOR DOUGH for illustration
and directions). Cover with cloth.

Deep-fry crescents, a few at a time, over medium-
low heat (325° F.) to an even golden brown, about
3 minutes, turning frequently with chopsticks.
Remove with slotted spoon and drain on absorbent
papers.

Deep-fried pastries freeze well. Reheat in slow
oven until soft. Read section on deep-frying for
complete frying directions.

鍋貼傺 POT STICKER ROLLS
makes 36

square won ton skins or paper-thin spring roll skins
cut into 4 equal squares
1 recipe CURRIED BEEF FILLING, page 83
1 can chicken broth or beef broth
dip of choice   oil for pan-frying
Paste: mix
       1 tablespoon all-purpose flour
   2-1/2 to 2-3/4 teaspoons water

Prepare filling as directed. Place a wrapper on the
kitchen counter with a corner pointing toward you and
lay a strip of filling across center. Starting from
the corner nearest you, fold it over the filling.
Moisten left and right corners with paste, then fold
in both corners. Roll up and moisten the last corner
to seal. Repeat process. Heat skillet. Add 2 tablespoons oil (add more as needed) and heat until hot.
Brown rolls on two sides over medium heat to get a
nice color. Remove excess oil from pan. Add 2/8" to
3/8" broth to pan. Cover and simmer until the liquid
has been absorbed but not dry, 2 to 3 minutes. Serve.
These mini rolls may be refrigerated or frozen. Wrap
in foil and reheat in slow oven until hot or reheat
over medium-low heat in a lightly oiled skillet with
very little liquid similar to the cooking method above.

GINGER BEEF ROLLS 薑肉捲
makes 20 mini rolls

蝦仁捲 SHRIMP ROLLS
makes 20 rolls

3/4 lb. flank steak, thinly sliced across grain & marinated in:

1-1/2 tablespoons cornstarch

1/2 teaspoon salt

1/8 teaspoon ground pepper

1 teaspoon *each* sesame oil and oil

1/2 tablespoon *each* cream sherry & dark soy sauce

1/4 cup slivered young spring ginger root

paper-thin spring roll skins, cut into 4 squares

oil for deep-frying   dip of choice

Paste: mix

1 tablespoon all-purpose flour

2-1/2 to 2-3/4 teaspoons water

Place a square of spring roll skin in front of you. Fill the side nearest you with two teaspoons beef and 3 or 4 ginger slivers. Roll up and seal the far side with paste. The finished roll has open ends. Place rolls on platter with seam side down. Proceed until all rolls are made. Deep-fry in 375° F. oil until golden, 1 minute or less, rolling frequently. Drain on absorbent toweling. Serve while crisp and hot. These mini rolls freeze well. Reheat in slow oven until hot and crisp.

20 (1/2 to 3/4 lb.) fresh medium prawns, shelled, deveined, cut in halves lengthwise, marinated in:

1/4 teaspoon salt

pinch of ground pepper

1/2 teaspoon *each* cornstarch, sesame oil and cream sherry

pinch of garlic powder or 1 small clove garlic, minced

1 teaspoon soy sauce

Paper-thin spring roll skins, cut into 4 squares

fresh coriander sprigs

oil for deep-frying   dip of choice

Paste: mix

1 tablespoon all-purpose flour

2-1/2 to 2-3/4 teaspoons water

Place a square of spring roll skin in front of you. Lay 2 half-prawns along the edge nearest you. Top with a coriander sprig or two. Roll up and seal the far edge with paste. The finished roll has open ends. Place roll on platter with seam side down. Proceed until all rolls are made. Deep-fry in 375° F. oil until golden, 1 minute or so, rolling frequently. Drain on absorbent papers. Serve. These rolls are excellent for hors d'oeuvres. The shrimp is tender and the green coriander shows through the wrapper.

VEGETARIAN SPRING ROLLS　齋喜捲
makes 16 rolls

2　slices fresh ginger

30　dried lily buds (golden needles), soaked to
　　soften, hard stems removed, squeezed dry,
　　cut in halves

10　dried Chinese mushrooms, soaked to soften,
　　stems removed, squeezed dry, cut in fine shreds

1/4　cup cloud ears, soaked to soften, hard stems
　　removed, squeezed dry, cut in fine shreds

6　sheets dried sweet bean curd, soaked to soften,
　　cut in fine shreds

1　cup finely shredded bamboo shoots

1　cup finely shredded broccoli or snow peas

1/2　cup water

1/2　lb. mung bean sprouts, rinsed and drained

1　tablespoon *each* soy sauce and oyster sauce

oil　　　　salt　　　　pepper

Mix:

　　2　tablespoons cornstarch

　　1　teaspoon chicken flavored stock base
　　　　(powder bouillon)

　　1/2　cup chicken broth

16　paper-thin spring roll skins

sweet and sour sauce or hot sauce for dip

Paste:　mix

　　1　tablespoon all-purpose flour

　2-1/2　to 2-3/4 teaspoons water

Preheat wok over high heat; add 2 tablespoons oil
and 1/2 teaspoon salt. When hot, add ginger and stir
until brown. Discard ginger. Add lily buds, mushrooms, cloud ears, bean curd, bamboo shoots and broccoli; stir-fry for 1 minute. Add water; cover and
cook for 1-1/2 minutes. Add cornstarch mixture and
stir until thickened. Remove from heat; add bean
sprouts. Season with soy sauce, oyster sauce, salt
(if needed) and pepper. Mix well and set aside.

Spread a wrapper on kitchen counter with a corner
pointing toward you, and lay a strip of filling
across center of the wrapper. Starting from the
corner nearest you, fold it over the filling and
roll over once. Moisten left and right corners with
paste, then fold in both corners. Roll up and moisten the last corner to seal. Deep-fry in 365° to
370° F. hot oil until golden brown, 1 to 2 minutes,
turning or rolling frequently. Drain on cake racks.
Cut each roll in fourths. While hot and crisp, serve
with dip.

Note. For homemade spring roll skins, see page 12.

BEAN-CURD ROLLS
makes about 12 rolls　　腐皮捲

4 oz. dried bean-curd sheets, soaked to soften
1 recipe BASIC PORK & SHRIMP FILLING, page 82
oil for deep-frying
Sauce: mix
    1/2 tablespoon cornstarch
    1/2 cup chicken broth
Paste:
    1 tablespoon cornstarch
    1 tablespoon water
    4 tablespoons boiling water

To make the paste: Mix cornstarch with 1 tablespoon cold water. Add to boiling water in a small saucepan; stir until thickened. Prepare filling.

Cut bean-curd sheets into 5"x5" squares, reserving leftovers for other uses (such as vegetarian dishes or soup). Pat dry with towel. Place a square on the counter with a corner pointing toward you and lay two tablespoons of filling across the square about 2-1/2" from this corner. Fold corner over to cover the filling, then roll over once. Fold in left and right corners, keeping corners in place with a little paste here and there. Roll up and seal the last corner with paste. Deep-fry in hot

oil until puffy, crisp and golden. (If the bean-curd wrapper is not puffy, but is smooth, the oil is not hot enough.) Drain on absorbent paper. Pour sauce into a skillet; cook and stir until thickened. There should be enough thin sauce to cover the bottom of the skillet. More broth or water can also be added later during cooking. Add fried bean-curd rolls. Cover and slow-simmer until the sauce is almost absorbed and the wrapper is soft. Serve hot.

Bean-curd rolls may be fried in advance, refrigerated or frozen, and simmered in sauce just before serving.

VARIATION: Omit the sauce and the simmering. Make crisp deep-fried bean-curd rolls with CURRIED BEEF FILLING or other cooked filling. Serve while crisp.

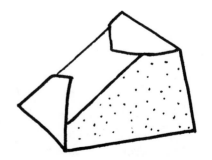 

1 recipe CHAR SHIU FILLING, page 81

oil for deep-frying

Taro Dough:

> 3 cups taro powder (similar to instant potato flakes in texture)
>
> 6 tablespoons lard *
>
> 3 tablespoons cornstarch
>
> 2 tablespoons sugar
>
> pinch of salt
>
> 1 cup to 17 tablespoons cold water

Prepare filling as directed. Place taro powder, lard, cornstarch, sugar and salt in a mixing bowl. Cut ingredients with two knives until fine. Gradually add water to form a dough and mix until smooth. The dough will resemble very dry mashed potato, somewhat crumbly. Divide dough into 12 equal portions. Pat a portion of dough with hands to make a 3-inch circle. Dot the center with 2 teaspoons filling. Fold circle in half to form a crescent. Pat and pinch edges to seal tightly. Deep-fry crescents, 2 or 3 at a time, in 365^0 to 370^0 F. oil (dough will "melt" at lower temperature and will burn at higher temperature) until golden, about 2 minutes.

Drain on absorbent papers. Bring oil back to the correct temperature before frying another batch. During the first minute of frying, do not roll or turn until the crescents are crusty.

Taro crescents freeze well. Reheat in slow oven until warm before serving.

* This is the secret for that honey-comb like texture on the outside crust.

CRISPY POTATO CRESCENTS
makes 8

脆皮薯角

1 recipe CURRIED BEEF FILLING, page 83
oil for deep-frying
Potato Dough:
  1-1/2 cups instant potato flakes
  1/4   teaspoon salt
  1   tablespoon sugar
  3   tablespoons cornstarch
  4   tablespoons lard or vegetable shortening
  1   cup water

Prepare filling as directed. In a heavy-bottomed 3-quart saucepan, bring water to a boil. Turn off heat. Add salt and potato flakes and stir to make well-mashed smooth potato. Cool. Add sugar, lard and cornstarch; mix until smooth. The dough should not be too dry or sticky. Divide dough into 8 portions. Pat each portion into a 3" circle and dot the center with 2 teaspoons filling. Fold circle in half. Pinch and pat to seal and form into crescent shape. Deep-fry, 2 or 3 crescents at a time, in 365° to 370° F. (dough will "melt" at lower temperature and will burn at higher temperature) oil until golden brown for 2 to 3 minutes. Drain on absorbent papers. Bring oil back to the correct temperature, then fry another batch. During the first minute of frying,

do not roll or turn until it is crusty.

These crescents can be refrigerated for a few days or frozen for a longer period. Reheat in slow oven until hot. Leftover filling can be used to make *won ton* or meat balls.

Dough A:

    1 cup all-purpose flour

    2 tablespoons shortening

    2 teaspoons sugar

    pinch of salt

3-1/2 tablespoons ice cold water

Dough B:

1/2 cup all-purpose flour

  2 tablespoons lard

  2 teaspoons ice cold water

To make dough A: Measure flour, shortening, sugar and salt into mixing bowl. Blend with pastry blender until fine. Gradually add water and knead several times to form somewhat a smooth dough. *DO NOT OVERWORK DOUGH.*

Repeat the above procedure with dough B. Dough B should be a little drier.

Divide each dough into 10 (12 or 15) equal pieces. Flatten a piece of dough A. Place a piece of dough B in the center and wrap around with dough A to form a ball. Roll out on smooth surface to a 1/8" to 1/4" thick rectangle. Then, starting with a short side, roll up into a stick. Turn stick so that one end points toward you, and roll out into a rectangle of 1"x5". Starting with a narrow end, fold up to get a 4-layered square. Keep covered.

Repeat until all squares are made. Now, the flaky pastry dough is ready to be rolled out into circles for filling.

This may sound time consuming, but the actual work goes quite fast. The resulting pastry is worth the effort.

The best way to roll out the dough is to: Roll out 2 or 3 times, turn dough over; roll out 2 or 3 times and turn dough over; etc. The dough rolls out much easier, resulting in flakier crust.

STUFFED FRESH MUSHROOMS 菇肉球
20-24 mushrooms

咖哩角 DEEP-FRIED CURRIED TURNOVERS
makes 15 crescents

3/4 lb. large (2"-2-1/2" across) mushrooms
 1 recipe Pork Filling, see STUFFED PRAWNS on
     page 77
all-purpose flour for dusting
coriander (Chinese parsley) for garnish
Serving accompaniment:

          soy sauce, mustard or chili oil

Prepare filling as directed. Wash mushrooms and
remove stems. Pat dry with paper toweling. Dust
the cavity of each mushroom with flour, then stuff
with filling. Arrange stuffed mushrooms, meat side
up, in a lightly greased heatproof plate. Steam
over boiling water until cooked through, about 18
minutes. Garnish with parsley. Serve hot with
or without accompaniment.

Stuffed fresh mushrooms may be prepared two days in
advance, cooked or uncooked. If cooked, reheat by
steaming until hot.

VARIATION: Stuff mushrooms with BASIC PORK & SHRIMP
FILLING.

 1 recipe FLAKY FRYING PASTRY DOUGH, page 54
 1 recipe CURRIED SEAFOOD FILLING, page 86
     or SPICY SHRIMP FILLING, page 86
oil for deep-frying

Prepare filling and dough as directed. Take a
square of dough and roll it out into a 3" circle.
Dot the center with 2 teaspoons filling. Fold circle
in half to form a crescent and seal edges. Crimp
sealed edges. See FUN GOR DOUGH for crimping directions. Repeat until all crescents are made. Deep-
fry crescents in 360° to 365° F. hot oil until
golden, about 3 minutes. Drain on absorbent paper.

Deep-fried pastries freeze well. Warm in slow oven,
then serve.

VARIATION: Make CURRIED BEEF TURNOVERS with CURRIED
BEEF FILLING.

BOILED DUMPLINGS IN SOUP 水餃湯
3 to 4 servings

雲吞湯 FRIED WON TON IN SOUP
6 to 8 servings

1   recipe BOILED DUMPLINGS WITH DIP, omitting dip, see page 30

Soup:

    1   13-3/4 oz. can clear chicken broth

  1/2   lb. napa cabbage, coarsely shredded

    2   cups water

      salt and soy sauce to taste

Prepare and cook dumplings as directed. Drain.
In a large saucepan, bring water and broth to
a full boil. Add cabbage and quickly bring it
back to a boil. Turn off heat, add dumplings,
salt and soy sauce. Give it a quick stir.
Serve immediately.

1   recipe FRIED CURRIED BEEF WON TON, page 46

1   whole chicken breast, skinned, boned, thinly sliced (less than 1/8" thick), marinated in:

    2   tablespoons cornstarch

  1/2   teaspoon salt

    2   teaspoons sherry

    1   teaspoon sesame oil

    1   tablespoon thin soy sauce

Soup:

    1   13-3/4 oz. can clear chicken broth

 3-1/2   cups water

  1/2   lb. napa cabbage, coarsely shredded

    1   tablespoon thin soy sauce

      salt to taste

Make and deep-fry won ton as directed. In a large
saucepan, bring water and broth to a full boil. Add
cabbage and quickly bring it back to a boil. Turn
heat off (electric stove) or to medium (gas stove);
add chicken and stir until chicken slices are tenderly cooked, about 40 seconds. Remove from heat. Add
soy sauce and salt. Drop won ton into soup and give
it a quick stir. Serve at once.

SIZZLING RICE SOUP 鍋巴湯
4 to 6 servings

2 cups cooked long grain rice, warm

oil for deep-frying

Soup:

- 10 raw medium-sized prawns, shelled, deveined and halved lengthwise
- 1/2 chicken breast, skinned, boned, cut in thin slices
- 1/4 lb. fresh mushrooms, thinly sliced with an egg slicer (this is the fast and easy way to slice mushrooms!)
- 1/4 lb. snow peas, diagonally diced (or use equal amount of green peas)
- 1 green onion, minced
- 1 13-3/4 oz. can chicken broth
- 3 cups water
- salt and pepper to taste

Marinade:

- 1/2 tablespoon cornstarch
- 1/8 teaspoon ground pepper
- 1/4 teaspoon salt
- 1 tablespoon thin soy sauce

Add marinade to prawns and chicken; mix and set aside. Wet hand. Pat the warm rice into a flat-bottomed baking pan to two-grain thickness. Bake in 250° F. oven until the rice kernels are dry, but not brown.

Break rice crust into 4" square pieces. Cool and store in closed canister until ready to fry.

Bring water and broth to a boil. Add mushrooms and peas and bring to a fast boil. Add prawns and chicken; stir to cook meat, 1 minute or less. Remove prawns, chicken and vegetables with slotted spoon and set aside.(This is to prevent overcooking; unless you have help, and the soup and the rice are ready to be put together at exactly the same moment.) Season soup with salt and pepper. Keep soup on hot stove awaiting the fried rice crust.

While preparing soup, heat oil to 365° to 375° F. Deep-fry rice crust until all kernels have puffed up, gently turning once. Remove with long handled wire skimmer. Immediately add to hot soup.(The soup should be very hot, but not boiling. If soup is not quite ready at this point, place fried rice in a hot bowl and keep it hot in the oven.) See and hear it sizzle! Return meat and vegetable to soup; add onion and stir. Serve *immediately*. For a spectacular show, make sure the soup and the rice are very hot. It is essential to prepare soup and rice simultaneously. Rice crust can also be dried in an uncovered skillet over stove.

TURKEY JOOK
enough rice soup for 6 to 10 servings

bones of 1 turkey, see below
1-1/4   cups long-grain rice
    1   slice fresh ginger
    1   13-3/4 oz. can clear chicken broth (or water)
    1   cup green peas, fresh or frozen
  1/2   red bell pepper, diced
    2   tablespoons thin soy sauce or to taste
    1   tablespoon sesame oil
  1/4   cup minced green onion
    2   to 3 cups minced (or diced) cooked turkey meat
    salt to taste
    shredded iceberg lettuce

In a large pot, add turkey bones to about 10 cups of
water. Bring to a boil, then simmer for about 30
minutes. Remove bones to plate. Pick out meat and
set aside. Pour broth through a strainer; discard
bones and residue. Add water to broth, if needed,
to measure 9 cups; set aside. In a large soup
kettle, wash rice several times. Add turkey broth,
ginger and let soak for two hours; then bring to a
boil. Reduce heat, cover and simmer 1-1/4 hours.
Pick out and discard ginger. Add chicken broth,
peas and red pepper. Quickly bring to a boil again.

Turn off heat. Add onion, sesame oil, soy sauce,
turkey meat and salt; stir. Ladle soup into bowls;
top with lettuce. Serve hot.

Jook can be served as *dim sum* or as a lazy summer
light supper. While *jook* is simmering, you can be
busy doing something else. It is also good if you
have a large piece of ham bone. There is no need
to cook ham bone in water first; simply add ham
bone to rice and cook as directed.

MO SHU PORK
fills 12-14 pancakes

木須肉

1/2 lb. (net weight) all lean boneless pork, coarsely shredded, marinated in:

    2 teaspoons cornstarch

    1/4 teaspoon salt

    2 teaspoons thin soy sauce

    1 teaspoon oil

1/2 lb. mung bean sprouts, rinsed and drained

15 dried lily buds (golden needles), soaked to soften, hard stems removed, squeezed dry, cut in halves

5 dried Chinese mushrooms, soaked to soften, hard stems removed, squeezed dry, cut in shreds

2 tablespoons cloud ears, soaked to soften, hard stems removed, squeezed dry, cut in shreds

1/4 cup shredded bamboo shoots (or 2 sheets dried sweet bean curd, soaked to soften, cut in shreds)

1 green onion, cut in 1" long thin strips

2 to 4 tablespoons hoisin sauce

oil for cooking

salt and ground pepper to taste

Mix:

    1 teaspoon cornstarch

    1/4 cup chicken broth

Heat wok, add 1-1/2 tablespoons oil and 1/4 teaspoon salt. When hot, add lily buds, mushrooms, cloud ears and bamboo shoots; stir until well coated with oil and very hot. Add 1/4 cup water. Cover and steam for 1-1/2 minutes. Add bean sprouts and stir-fry 1 to 1-1/2 minutes. Season with pepper to taste. Remove and set aside.

Reheat wok; stir-fry pork in 1-1/2 tablespoons hot oil until well done. Add cornstarch mixture; stir until thickened. Add onion and remove wok from heat. Toss in vegetables. Add more salt or soy sauce, if desired. Serve with MANDARIN PANCAKES, page 40.

Spread hoisin sauce on a pancake, fill with some *mo shu pork*, fold or roll up, and eat!

Mo shu pork can also be served with egg crêpes instead of pancakes. Or, as a meat and vegetable dish for dinner.

VARIATION: Make MO SHU CHICKEN, substituting chicken meat for pork.

4 squares (approximately 4"x4"x1" each) pressed
   fresh bean-curd cake, well drained
1 recipe BASIC PORK & SHRIMP FILLING, page 82
oyster sauce or soy sauce
ground pepper
sesame oil
salt

Diagonally cut each block of bean-curd cake into 2
triangles. Cut a "pocket" along the longest side
(for you mathematicians, it is the hypotenuse of
this right triangle) by removing a small portion of
the bean curd in the center; do not cut through the
other two sides. Prepare filling as directed.
Stuff "pockets" with filling. Arrange triangles in
a single layer on heatproof plate. Sprinkle surfaces
with a little salt. Steam over gently boiling water
until filling is cooked. Pour off excess liquid,
then sprinkle tops with a few drops of sauce, pinch
of ground pepper and a few drops of sesame oil.
Serve hot.

VARIATION # 1: Coat a preheated skillet with a

small amount of oil. Lightly brown bean-curd triangles on both sides. Add 3/4 cup chicken broth
(or water) mixed with 1/2 tablespoon cornstarch;
cover and simmer until the filling is cooked, adding more water if needed. Garnish with coriander
and serve hot.

VARIATION # 2: Purchase deep-fried triangular
shaped bean curd. Stuff as directed above and
cook as in variation #1. Deep-fried bean curd
can be frozen, if necessary.

Fresh bean curd should be eaten as soon as possible.
Leftovers should be refrigerated. It will keep for
one or two days, however.

ANTS CLIMBING TREE
6 servings

蚂蟻上樹

1   lb. ground pork (or beef), marinated in:

   2   pinches chili powder

   4   teaspoons cornstarch

 1/2   teaspoon salt

   2   teaspoons *each* thin soy sauce, sesame oil
      and cooking oil

   1   teaspoon hoisin sauce

2   oz. vermicelli (bean threads/cellophane noodles),
   loosened and divided into 4 parts

2   green onions, minced

oil for cooking

Mix:

   1   cup chicken or beef broth

   4   teaspoons cornstarch

Taking one part of threads at a time, lower into 365°
F. hot oil and immediately turn it over to fry until
puffy and expanded. This takes only a few seconds.
Repeat with remaining parts.

In a preheated wok, heat 2 tablespoons oil until hot;
add meat and stir-fry over high heat until done.
Pour off excess oil. Add cornstarch mixture; stir
until thickened. Remove from heat and add onions;

mix well. Line a serving platter with fried noodles
and top with meat mixture. Serve at once.

Noodles can be fried in advance and stored in air-
tight container, and the meat can be marinated overnight.

Despite its unappetizing name, *ants climbing tree*
is a delicious dish. The deep-fried vermicelli
melt in the mouth.

CHAR SHIU CHOW FUN
4 to 6 servings
义烧炒粉

2 lbs. fresh rice noodles, homemade (see RICE NOODLE ROLLS WITH SPICY BEEF FILLING) or store bought

1/2 lb. *char shiu* (homemade or store bought), sliced

2 oz. Chinese chives, cut in 1" lengths

1/2 bunch broccoli

1 tablespoon *each* oyster sauce & dark soy sauce

1/2 teaspoon sesame oil

salt and pepper

oil

Reheat wok and coat it with 1 to 1-1/2 tablespoons oil. Add noodles; gently toss and turn until hot. (If noodles were chilled and hard, steam until hot and soft. Omit the oil and the toss and turn heating process described in this paragraph. Just add noodles to the wok. For a lower fat content, steaming is recommended.) Turn off heat, add meat, vegetables, oyster sauce, soy sauce and sesame oil; mix well. Season with salt and pepper to taste. Serve. *Chow fun* is best when eaten fresh and hot.

For the broccoli: Peel off the outer tough covering along the lower part of the main stems. Cut diagonally--julienne style.

Coat a preheated wok with as little oil as possible. When hot, add *char shiu* and stir only to heat through. Remove and set aside.

Heat wok again, stir-fry broccoli in 1 tablespoon hot oil for 2 minutes, adding a little salt and sprinkling 1 to 2 tablespoons of water as needed. Add chives and continue to stir-fry for another minute. Spoon over meat.

RICE NOODLE ROLLS WITH SPICY BEEF FILLING
makes 10 rolls

Dough: combine ingredients and beat until smooth

    2 cups **sifted cake flour**

    2 tablespoons oil

    1 teaspoon salt

1-1/2 cups **cold water**

Spicy Beef Filling:

    2 carrots, shaved (peel with potato peeler to resemble shreds)

1/2 lb. beef, shredded, and marinated in:

      2 teaspoons grated fresh ginger

      2 tablespoons cornstarch

    1/4 teaspoon ground pepper

    1/4 teaspoon salt

      1 teaspoon sesame oil

1-1/2 tablespoons teriyaki barbecue marinade and sauce

Thickener: blend

    1/8 teaspoon salt

      1 tablespoon cornstarch

    1/4 cup clear beef broth

soy sauce or oyster sauce for dip

oil for cooking

Stir-fry carrots in 1 tablespoon hot oil for two minutes, adding 1 tablespoon water. Add cornstarch mixture and stir until thickened. Set aside.

Reheat wok and add 1-1/2 tablespoons oil. When oil is hot, stir-fry beef until just tenderly cooked, 1 to 1-1/2 minutes. Remove from heat, add carrots and mix well.

Lightly brush oil over bottom and sides of an 8"x8" teflon-coated pan. Pour 4 tablespoons batter into pan. Tilt to coat evenly while pan is floating over hot water in a 12" or 14" skillet. Cover and steam until cooked, about 3 minutes. Remove pan from steaming water. Run spatula or chopstick around sides of pan to loosen noodle and lay a strip of filling across the center; roll up. Place rolled noodle seam side down on lightly oiled platter. Repeat until batter is all used. Cut rolls into 6 pieces. Serve with dip.

TO MAKE PLAIN RICE NOODLES: Omit filling. Make rice noodles as directed above. Roll up. Cut into noodle-sized strips for CHAR SHIU CHOW FUN. Or, cut into 6 equal pieces and serve with soy sauce for dip.

SUBGUM WAR MEIN
4 to 6 servings

什錦窩麵

1 lb. fresh wide noodles or 1/2 lb. dried wide noodles (*war mein* type)

1/4 lb. fresh medium prawns, shelled, deveined & cut lengthwise in halves

1/2 chicken breast, skinned, boned & thinly sliced

1/4 lb. lean pork, thinly sliced

1 small bunch Chinese chives or 2 green onions, cut in 1" lengths

1 small carrot, shredded

2 oz. fresh mushrooms, sliced with egg slicer

1 13-3/4 oz. can chicken broth or other stock

3 cups water for soup

1 tablespoon thin soy sauce

salt and pepper to taste

Marinade: mix

  2 teaspoons cornstarch

  3/4 teaspoon salt

  1 teaspoon *each* oil, sesame oil & sherry

  1/8 teaspoon *each* ground ginger & ground pepper

  2 teaspoons thin soy sauce

Add marinade to prawns, chicken and pork; mix well and set aside.

Cook noodles in a large pot of rapidly boiling water, uncovered, until just tender. The number of minutes required to cook the noodles will depend on the type of noodles. Fresh noodles take about 3 minutes; dried noodles take about 5 minutes or longer. Drain. Rinse with cold water. Drain again.

Over high heat, bring broth and water to a boil. Add chives, carrot and mushrooms and bring it back to a fast rapid boil. Turn heat lower (gas stove) or off (electric stove), then add meats; stir until cooked, about a minute. Return noodles to the pot and season with soy sauce, salt (about 1/2 teaspoon) and pepper. Serve at once.

SHREDDED PORK CHOW MEIN
6 to 10 servings 肉絲炒麵

1   lb. fresh Chinese-style noodles
1/2   lb. lean pork, shredded, marinated in:
  1/2   teaspoon salt
    1   tablespoon cornstarch
  1/2   tablespoon thin soy sauce
    1   teaspoon *each* sesame oil & cream sherry
1/2   lb. snow peas, ends and strings removed, cut
      diagonally into 1/4" strips
  1   slice fresh ginger
1/4   lb. fresh mushrooms, sliced
1/2   lb. mung bean sprouts
  1   tablespoon dark soy sauce
  2   tablespoons oyster sauce
  1   teaspoon sesame oil
oil for cooking
salt & pepper to taste
Mix:
  1/2   tablespoon cornstarch
  1/2   cup chicken broth or other stock

In a large pot, add noodles to rapidly boiling water.
Cook, uncovered, 3 minutes. Drain, rinse with cold
water, mix with 1 tablespoon oil and drain until
dry (no more water dripping out). In a preheated

large wok, heat 1 to 2 tablespoons oil. When hot,
spread half of the noodles over bottom and fry over
medium to medium-high heat until the underside is
golden brown, occasionally sprinkling 1 or 2 tablespoons water over noodles so that noodles won't be
too dry and will still turn golden brown. Turn over
and brown the other side in the same manner. Transfer
noodles to a saucepan. Keep warm in oven. Repeat
with remaining noodles. Reheat wok and stir-fry pork
in 1 tablespoon hot oil until thoroughly cooked. Set
aside. Again, heat wok with 1 to 2 tablespoons oil.
Add ginger; stir until pungent. Add peas; stir-fry
for 1 minute, sprinkling 1 to 2 tablespoons water as
needed to create steam and sizzle. Add mushrooms.
After stirring around several times, add bean sprouts
and stir-fry for 1 minute, seasoning vegetables with
a little salt as you cook. Spoon vegetables over
meat, leaving liquid (if any) in the wok. Pour cornstarch mixture into wok (add 1/4 cup more broth if
there is no liquid in the wok); stir and cook until
translucent. Turn off heat. Return noodles, meat
and vegetables to wok and quickly toss to mix. Season
with soy sauce, oyster sauce, salt, sesame oil and
pepper. Serve immediately.

SWEET RICE WITH CHICKEN WRAPPED IN LOTUS LEAF

makes 8 nor mei gai

糯米雞

3   cups sweet rice (glutinous rice)

8   lotus leaves

1/2 lb. *char shiu*, cut in 1" chunks

8   roasted ready-to-eat chestnuts (if available), halved

8   dried Chinese mushrooms, soaked to soften, stems removed, sliced

1/2 chicken breast, boned, skinned, cut in 1" chunks, marinated in:

- 1/2   teaspoon cornstarch
- 1/8   teaspoon salt
- pinch of white pepper
- 1/2   tablespoon thin soy sauce

Sauce: mix

- 1/4   lb. ground pork
- 1/4   cup minced bamboo shoots
- 1   tablespoon cornstarch
- 1/2   cup chicken broth

oil for cooking

salt

thin soy sauce

ground pepper

Wash and soak rice overnight. Place rice in a fine-mesh colander and make a "well" in the center. Set colander on high rack above water in a large pot. Cover and bring to a boil; reduce heat and steam 25 to 30 minutes until rice is completely cooked, sprinkling 1/2 cup of water over the rice sometime during cooking. Season with salt and soy sauce to taste. This part can be done in advance; refrigerate rice in closed container.

Soak leaves, wash thoroughly and rinse. Boil leaves for 10 minutes, then soak in cold water. Advance preparation is advised. When ready to use, drain and shake off excess water.

Stir-fry chicken in 1-1/2 tablespoons hot oil only to cook through, about 3 minutes. Spoon over *char shiu*. Add mushrooms and sauce mixture to pan and cook until pork is done. Season with salt, pepper and soy sauce to taste. Mix in *char shiu* and chicken. Cool or keep in refrigerator until ready to wrap.

Lay a leaf on counter. With wet hands, spread 1/2 cup rice on the best side of leaf to cover a 4"x4" area. Top with 1/8 filling and 2 chestnut halves,

and cover filling with another 1/2 cup rice. Fold
up to enclose contents. Repeat wrapping as above
until all 8 *nor mei gai* are made. Place in steamer
with the seam side down. Steam over boiling water
for 1-1/2 hours. The leaves will impart a delicious
and unique flavor to the contents. Refrigerate or
freeze extra *nor mei gai*. Steam before serving.

牛肉球　　TENDER CURRIED MEAT BALLS
　　　　　　　16 to 20 meat balls

1 recipe CURRIED BEEF FILLING, page 83
tender parts of watercress or spinach, washed
a small piece of red bell pepper, shredded

Prepare meat as directed. Make meat balls, using
approximately 2 tablespoons of meat mixture for each.
Line a heatproof plate with a handful of greens and
place meat balls on top, then garnish with pepper.
Steam over barely simmering water just until cooked
through, about 12 minutes. Serve hot.

The secret of steaming beef so that it is juicy and
tender is to keep the water below the bubbling point.

Meat balls can be cooked one or two days in advance
and refrigerated. Steam until hot, then serve.

YANGCHOW FRIED RICE
6 to 10 servings

揚州炒飯

6 cups cooked rice

1/2 lb. cooked shrimp meat

1 cup diced cooked meat (chicken, ham, pork or turkey ham)

10 water chestnuts, diced

1 cup frozen green peas, thawed

1 2-1/2 oz. can mushrooms, diced

2 green onions, minced

1 tablespoon *each* dark soy sauce & oyster sauce

1 teaspoon sesame oil

salt and ground pepper to taste

oil

Mix:

1 teaspoon sherry

1 teaspoon light soy sauce

Beat:

2 eggs

pinch of ground pepper

pinch of salt

Heat 2 tablespoons oil in a preheated wok until hot. Add eggs and make scrambled eggs. Cut into bits with the wok spatula as you turn and stir. Remove and set aside.

Add 1-1/2 tablespoons oil to wok. When hot, add shrimp. Stir-fry until the wok gets dry. Drizzle sherry-soy over and let it sizzle for a few seconds. Spoon over eggs.

Again, add 2 tablespoons oil to wok and wait until it is hot. Add water chestnuts, peas and mushrooms; stir-fry until peas are cooked through. Spoon over shrimp. Add rice and meat to wok and stir-fry until very hot. Return shrimp, eggs, vegetables to rice; add onions and season with soy sauce, oyster sauce, sesame oil, salt and pepper. Mix well and serve hot.

GOLD COIN PORK
25 to 30 gold coins

壹錢肉

1-1/2 lbs. (net weight after cutting, see below) pork or beef

Marinade:

   1/2   teaspoon salt

   1/8   teaspoon *each* ground pepper & ground ginger

 1-1/2   tablespoons cornstarch

    2   tablespoons Chinese barbecue sauce

   1/2   tablespoon cream sherry

    1   teaspoon sesame oil

Sauce: mix

    1   tablespoon Chinese barbecue sauce

   1/2   tablespoon dark soy sauce

    1   teaspoon oil

    2   tablespoons warm water

garnish, see FANCY GARNISHES

Cut meat across the grain in 2-1/2" rounds having 1/4" thickness. Save the scraps for a stir-fry dish. Marinate meat for at least 2 hours or overnight for advance preparation.

Skewer meat onto rotisserie. Roast at 350° F. in the oven (about 30 minutes for pork) or barbecue over open fire until the meat is done. Remove meat to

platter. Arrange "coins" in rows. "Coins" should be placed at an angle and partially overlapping. Drip sauce all over meat and garnish. Serve warm or cold, with or without CRESCENT SHAPED STEAMED BUNS.

To reheat, wrap in foil and warm in the oven.

Note. Gold coin pork is usually made sandwich-style with a piece of pork fat between two slices of lean meat. The above is a modified low-fat version.

Chinese-style glazed roasted pork strips

3 lbs. (trimmed weight) lean boneless pork

3 tablespoons Chinese barbecue sauce

1-1/2 teaspoons salt

1/4 teaspoon ground pepper

1/4 teaspoon ground ginger

1 tablespoon sherry

1 teaspoon sesame oil

Honey Glaze: mix well in a large bowl

2 tablespoons honey

1 tablespoon dark soy sauce

Cut meat along grain into strips about 8" long with a cross section approximately 2"x2". Combine the barbecue sauce, salt, pepper, ginger, sherry and sesame oil and pour over meat; mix well. Let marinate at least three hours or overnight. Arrange meat strips in a single layer on an oven rack. Place a large roasting pan, filled with 1/4" water, 4 to 6 inches below the rack. Roast at 375° F. for 30 minutes. Turn strips over and roast about 25 minutes more or until both sides are lightly brown and the meat is cooked through. Do not overcook. Add hot meat to honey glaze; toss and coat well. Slice meat strips and arrange

on platter. Pour remaining glaze, if any, over meat and serve. Extra strips can be refrigerated in a plastic container for about 5 days or frozen for a longer period.

Char shiu can be purchased from Chinese markets as well as delicatessens. It is the "all purpose" roasted meat. It makes an excellent filling and it is often added to vegetable or noodle dishes. Try a *char shiu* sandwich.

PEPPER AND STEAK CUBES
about 30 pieces

煎肉片

1/2 *each* green and red bell pepper, cut in 1"
     squares

  2 slices fresh ginger

oil   salt   colored picks

3/4 lb. New York cut, top sirloin or London broil,
     cut into 1-1/2"x1-1/2"x1/4" pieces, marinated
     in:

   1/4 teaspoon salt

   1/8 teaspoon ground pepper

     1 teaspoon *each* cornstarch, sesame oil
        and sherry

     1 tablespoon Chinese barbecue sauce

Heat wok, then add 1/2 tablespoon oil. When oil is
hot, stir-fry red and green pepper for about 1-1/2
minutes. Add salt to taste. Remove and set aside.
Again, heat wok, then add 1 to 1-1/2 tablespoons oil.
When oil has reached the sizzling point, add ginger
and stir to extract flavor. Brown meat, a few pieces
at a time, on both sides to desired doneness, adding
more oil as needed. Serve as a meat dish. Or,
spear a slice each of red pepper, meat and green
pepper on a pick. Serve as hors d'oeuvres.

红烧鸭

RED DUCK
a scrumptious dish

  1 4-5 lbs. ready-to-cook duckling

1/2 to 1 sweet Spanish onion, cut in big slices

  1 whole (or 8-10 pods) star anise

Sauce: mix

     1 tablespoon brown sugar

     2 tablespoons cream sherry

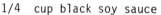

   1/4 cup black soy sauce

     1 tablespoon fermented red bean curd (nam yu)

     1 tablespoon red bean curd sauce (from red
        bean curd)

   1/2 cup water, add more if needed during cooking
garnish, see FANCY GARNISHES

Bring a large pot of water to a boil. Immerse duck
in boiling water for 3-4 minutes, turning often. Remove duck and discard the hot water. Place onion,
star anise and sauce in a large heavy-bottomed pot;
bring to a boil. Add duck, cover and bring to a
boil. Reduce heat to medium and cook for 1-1/2
hours or until tender, turning and basting duck with
the sauce occasionally. If necessary, reduce heat
to a lower temperature during the last half hour of
cooking. The duck should be tender, the skin should
be dark brown, and the sauce is thickened. Chop duck.
Pour sauce over duck, garnish, and serve.

CRISPY DUCK

a supreme delicacy

脆皮鴨

茶葉蛋

TEA EGGS

6 eggs

one 4 to 5 lbs. duckling, cleaned & well-drained

2   tablespoons thin soy sauce

2   tablespoons water chestnut powder

oil for deep-frying

SZECHWAN PEPPER SALT, page 108

Marinade: mix

      2-1/2   teaspoons salt

      1/2   teaspoon *each* ground pepper, ground
           ginger and Chinese 5-spice

Rub the inside and the outside of the duck with the
marinade; let stand in refrigerator overnight.
Place duck in a large shallow heatproof plate or
steamer; steam over boiling water for 1 hour and
45 minutes. Cool duck until warm. Rub thin soy
sauce over the exterior of the duck; let stand to
dry for 2 hours. Then, work the water chestnut
powder all over and into the duck skin. Let stand
30 minutes or more. Heat oil to 375° to 380° F.
Deep-fry the duck for 5 minutes, turning once. Remove duck. Reheat oil. Deep-fry duck again until
crisp for another 3 to 5 minutes, turning once or
twice. Cool. Cut into segments; serve with spiced
salt. Or, bone the duck, serve with MANDARIN PAN-
CAKES or CRESCENT-SHAPED STEAMED BUNS.

6   eggs, hard boiled, rinsed with cold water, cooled

2   tablespoons black tea leaves or 2 tea bags

1   tablespoon salt

3   whole star anise

2   tablespoons dark soy sauce

2   to 2-1/2 cups water

Gently crack eggs, but do not shell. Place eggs and
other ingredients in pan; add water to cover. Bring
to a boil, then simmer for an hour. Let stand in
liquid for an hour. The sauce pentrates through the
cracks, creating an antique porcelain appearance.
Serve warm or cold. Leftover eggs should be kept in
the refrigerator. Shell eggs just before serving.

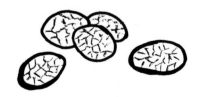

CRISP SOY SAUCE SQUABS
2-4 servings

香酥豉油鴿

2   ready-to-cook squabs or Rock Cornish game hens

oil for deep-frying

sweet and sour duck sauce for dip

Sauce: mix as much as needed in the following
        proportion

    1/4   cup brown sugar

    1/2   teaspoon Chinese 5-spice

    1/4   (2 pods) star anise

      1   teaspoon salt

      1   cup dark soy sauce

      1   cup water

Mix:

      2   tablespoons water chestnut flour

    2-1/2 teaspoons water

    1/2   teaspoon honey

Fill a deep saucepan with enough sauce to cover
squabs, but not more than half-full. Soy sauce
boils over easily. Bring sauce to a boil. Add
squabs. When sauce begins to boil, adjust heat to
keep the sauce just below the boiling point. The
sauce should barely simmer. Turn squabs over once
or twice. Simmer for 30 minutes. Remove saucepan
from heat. Let stand for an hour (birds can be

served at this stage as soy sauce squabs). Lift
out birds, drain, cool, then let dry for 2 to 3
hours. For advance preparation, leave birds in
refrigerator to dry overnight. Store sauce in
refrigerator; use it to cook other meats, vegetables
and gravy. Rub the outside of the birds with the
honey mixture. Deep-fry in hot (375^0 F.) oil until
golden and crisp, about 5 minutes, turning frequently. Drain. Serve whole, halved or cut up. When
garnished, it makes an elegant entree for two. Or,
bone the birds, serve them Peking duck-style with
MANDARIN PANCAKES or CRESCENT-SHAPED STEAMED BUNS.

GARLICKY CHICKEN WINGS
10 chicken wings

蒜汁雞翼

10 (1 package) chicken wings, tips removed, cut at joints, and marinated in:

    2 small (or 1 large) cloves garlic, minced

    2 thin slices fresh ginger, minced

  1/4 heaping teaspoon Chinese 5-spice

  1/2 teaspoon salt

    1 tablespoon sherry

    1 tablespoon teriyaki barbecue marinade & sauce

2 tablespoons cornstarch

oil for deep-frying

coriander sprig for garnish

Sauce:

    2 teaspoons oil

    1 clove garlic, finely minced

Mix:

    1 teaspoon brown sugar

    1 tablespoon white vinegar

    1 tablespoon reserved marinade, see below

Let chicken pieces marinate for several hours or overnight. Sprinkle the inside of a plastic bag with cornstarch; add chicken, reserving 1 tablespoon marinade (if there is not enough, "wash" the bowl and add to the marinade to measure 1 tablespoon). Close plastic bag and shake to coat chicken with cornstarch. Let stand for 10 to 15 minutes. Deep-fry chicken at 365° F. until golden brown, crisp and cooked through, 4 to 5 minutes. Drain on absorbent papers, then transfer to serving platter.

To make the sauce: Heat 2 teaspoons oil in a heavy small saucepan until very hot. Add garlic and stir only to coat with oil. Immediately pour in vinegar mixture to let it sizzle for a few seconds. Drizzle over chicken. Garnish and serve for *dim sum* or dinner.

CRISP DEEP-FRIED DRUMSTICKS
12 drumsticks

炸雞腿

12 frying chicken drumsticks
1/2 teaspoon Chinese 5-spice
1/2 teaspoon salt
1 teaspoon sesame oil
1/2 teaspoon minced fresh ginger
1 tablespoon soy sauce
oil for deep-frying
Coating: mix
     6 tablespoons tempura batter mix
  1/8 teaspoon *each* salt and ground pepper
     4 tablespoons water

Marinate chicken in 5-spice, salt, sesame oil, ginger and soy sauce for a few hours or overnight.

Coat drumsticks with batter mix. Deep-fry in 375° F. hot oil until golden and cooked through. Drain on rack or absorbent papers. Serve hot or cold.

紅燒雞

RED-COOKED DRUMSTICKS
12 drumsticks

12 frying chicken drumsticks
2 slices ginger
1/4 teaspoon *each* salt and pepper
2 tablespoons *each* dark soy sauce and oyster sauce
1 tablespoon sherry
1/2 cup water
garnish, see FANCY GARNISHES
oil for cooking

In a large heavy-bottomed pan, brown chicken in two tablespoons hot oil with the ginger. Drain off the excess oil, then add remaining ingredients. Cover and simmer for 30 minutes until tender, turning drumsticks over frequently to get a nice even "red" color. If there is too much liquid in the pan, uncover, and cook over high heat until a gravy consistency remains. Garnish and serve.

Drumsticks can be cooked 3 days in advance and kept in refrigerator. Add a small amount of water or broth and reheat until hot.

HOT AND SPICY PRAWNS
酸辣蝦
2 or 3 servings

1/2 lb. raw medium-sized prawns, shelled, deveined, leaving tail segments intact, marinated in:

- 1/8 teaspoon salt
- 1 tablespoon tempura batter mix
- 1 clove garlic, minced
- 1 slice ginger, minced
- 1/2 tablespoon thin soy sauce
- 1 teaspoon cream sherry

Sauce: mix

- 1/2 tablespoon cornstarch
- 1/8 teaspoon salt
- 1-1/2 tablespoons white vinegar
- 2-1/2 teaspoons brown sugar
- 2 teaspoons ground bean sauce
- 1 teaspoon sesame oil
- 1/8 teaspoon chili powder
- 1/4 cup water

1 green onion, minced

oil for deep-frying

Drop prawns, one by one, into hot oil; deep-fry until golden brown, 3 to 5 minutes. Drain, then transfer to server. In a small saucepan, cook sauce until thickened. Mix in green onion and pour over prawns. Serve hot.

SWEET AND SOUR PRAWNS
甜酸蝦
2 or 3 servings

1/2 lb. raw medium-sized prawns, shelled, deveined, leaving tail segments intact, marinated in:

- 1/8 teaspoon salt
- 1 tablespoon tempura batter mix
- 1 clove garlic, minced
- 1 slice ginger, minced
- 1/2 tablespoon thin soy sauce
- 1 teaspoon cream sherry

Sauce: mix

- 1/2 tablespoon cornstarch
- 1/8 teaspoon salt
- 1 teaspoon brown sugar
- 1 tablespoon white vinegar
- 1/4 cup pineapple syrup (from canned pineapple)
- 10 to 12 pieces pineapple chunks
- 1-1/2 tablespoons tomato catsup
- 1 teaspoon oil

oil for deep-frying

Drop prawns, one by one, into hot oil; deep-fry until golden brown, 3 to 5 minutes. Drain, then transfer to server. In a small saucepan, cook sauce until clear and thickened. Pour over prawns. Serve hot.

STUFFED PRAWNS
16 to 18 stuffed prawns

蝦 球

all-purpose flour for dusting

oil for cooking

16 to 18 (1/2 lb.) raw medium-sized prawns, shelled
   and deveined

Marinade: mix

    1/4 scant teaspoon salt

    1/2 teaspoon sesame oil

    1/2 teaspoon cream sherry

      1 teaspoon teriyaki barbecue marinade
         and sauce

    pinch of ground pepper

Pork Filling: mix

    1/2 lb. ground pork

      1 slice ginger, finely minced

      1 green onion, minced

      2 dried Chinese mushrooms, soaked to
         soften and minced

    1/8 teaspoon ground pepper

      4 teaspoons cornstarch

    1/4 teaspoon salt

      1 tablespoon teriyaki barbecue marinade
         and sauce

Dip: mustard, chili oil or a mixture of chili oil,
     vinegar and soy sauce

Slit prawns lengthwise, but do not cut through, and
flatten. Marinate for a few hours or overnight.
Dust the inner side of each prawn with flour.
Spread and press 2 to 3 teaspoons filling onto the
floured tops. Heat skillet until hot; add 2 tablespoons oil. When oil is hot, add stuffed prawns.
Pan-fry over medium-low heat for 5 to 7 minutes or
until both sides are golden brown and cooked
through, turning frequently. Serve hot with or
without dip.

Stuffed prawns can be refrigerated or frozen. Reheat
in oven until hot, then serve.

DEEP-FRIED OYSTERS 炸生蠔
about 20 oysters

20 oz. (2 jars) fresh small oysters, cleaned, drained and marinated in:

- 1/4 teaspoon salt
- 1/8 teaspoon ground pepper
- 2 slices ginger, minced
- 1 clove garlic, minced
- 1 teaspoon *each* hoisin sauce, sesame oil and soy sauce

1 small green onion, minced
1/2 cup all-purpose flour
1/2 teaspoon baking powder
1 egg, beaten slightly
oil for deep-frying
lemon wedges

Gently toss oysters and marinate overnight in refrigerator. Add flour, baking powder, onion and egg to oysters. Gently stir to mix. Heat oil for deep-frying. Spoon each oyster with some marinade into hot fat and deep-fry until golden brown, turning occasionally. Drain on absorbent toweling. Serve hot with or without lemon wedges.

鮑魚 OYSTER FLAVORED ABALONE
a seafood delicacy

1 can (16 oz.) abalone
3 thin slices fresh ginger, shredded
green onion or coriander, cut in 1" lengths
cocktail picks
oil for cooking
Mix:

- 1/2 teaspoon sugar
- 2 tablespoons oyster sauce
- 1 tablespoon sherry
- 1 teaspoon sesame oil

Empty abalone and liquid into a pot having a tight lid. Bring to a boil, then simmer until tender (1/2 to 2 hours, depending on quality of abalone). Discard liquid and slice abalone as thinly as possible. Heat wok until hot; add 1 tablespoon oil. When oil is hot, add ginger; stir to brown and extract flavor. Pick out and discard ginger, if desired. Pour sauce mixture into hot ginger oil and let it sizzle for a second or two. Remove from heat. Toss in abalone and onion. Serve hot as a seafood dish or serve with colored picks for hors d'oeuvres.

Additional Filling Recipes

CRISPY DUCK, page 72

SAVORY FLAKY TRIANGLES, page 30

FAN-SHAPED STEAMED BUNS, page 32

SHRIMP ROLLS, page 49

CHAR SHIU FILLING 叉燒餡　　葱肉餡 CHAR SHIU WITH ONION FILLING

1/2　lb. *char shiu* (Chinese-style glazed roasted pork strips), minced

1-1/2　tablespoons cornstarch

1　tablespoon sugar

3/4　cup water

1　teaspoon sesame oil

1　tablespoon oyster sauce

1/2　tablespoon soy sauce

pinch ground pepper

2　tablespoons finely chopped coriander

Heat **sugar and half the water** until hot. Add mixture of cornstarch and remaining water; stir until thickened. Season with sesame oil, oyster sauce, soy sauce and pepper. Toss in meat and coriander. Remove to let cool.

Refrigerate or freeze leftover filling.

1　lb. coarsely minced *char shiu*, homemade or store bought

3/4　to 1 cup (1 medium) chopped onion (sweet Spanish onion)

2　tablespoons oyster sauce

1/8　teaspoon ground pepper

2　tablespoons oil

Mix:

1　tablespoon cornstarch

6　tablespoons water

Stir-fry onion in 2 tablespoons hot oil until limp. Add cornstarch mixture; stir until thickened. Add meat, oyster sauce and pepper; mix well. Cool.

For advance preparation, refrigerate or freeze filling.

GROUND PORK FILLING　猪肉餡

Mix together:

- 1/2 lb. lean ground pork, see ground pork, page 8
- 2 tablespoons minced green onion

pinch of grated fresh orange peel*

- 1/2 cup chopped canned mushrooms
- 1-1/2 tablespoons cornstarch
- 1/2 teaspoon salt
- 1 tablespoon oyster sauce
- 1/2 teaspoon sesame oil
- 2 teaspoons cream sherry

* Do not grate with the grater. Using a potato peeler, peel 2 slices of skin off an orange, then chop with cleaver until fine as granulated sugar. Dried Chinese tangerine peel can also be used. Soak to soften, then chop as directed above.

蝦仁餡　BASIC PORK & SHRIMP FILLING

Mix together:

- 1/2 lb. ground pork
- 1/2 lb. raw medium-sized prawns, shelled, deveined and diced
- 6 dried Chinese mushrooms, soaked to soften, minced
- 10 water chestnuts, minced (or 1/4 cup minced bamboo shoots)
- 2 tablespoons cornstarch
- 1/2 teaspoon salt
- 1/8 teaspoon *each* ground ginger and pepper
- 1 tablespoon *each* oyster sauce and fish sauce (or soy sauce)
- 1/2 tablespoon *each* sesame oil and sherry
- 1/4 cup minced green onion/Chinese chives/coriander

For advance preparation, refrigerate or freeze filling. Very finely minced fresh ginger root may be substituted for ground ginger.

STIR-FRIED PORK FILLING 炒肉餡　　牛肉餡 CURRIED BEEF FILLING

1 lb. coarsely minced lean pork (do not use over-the-counter ground pork), marinated in:

    1 tablespoon cornstarch

    1/2 teaspoon salt

    1 teaspoon chicken flavored stock base (powder chicken bouillon)

    2 thin slices ginger, minced

    1 tablespoon dark soy sauce

    1 tablespoon oil

Mix:

    2 teaspoons cornstarch

    1 tablespoon oyster sauce

    1/4 cup chicken broth

1/2 cup minced green onion

oil for cooking

Heat wok. Add 2 tablespoons oil. When oil is hot, add meat; stir-fry until cooked through, 3 to 4 minutes. Add cornstarch mixture; stir until thickened. Add onion; stir and set aside to cool. Total cooking time is about 5 minutes. This filling is good for biscuits, baked dumplings, and completely sealed dumplings to be deep-fried. It may be refrigerated for 2 days or frozen. If frozen, thaw, then use as directed.

Mix:

    1 lb. all lean beef* (top round or better), minced

    2 thin slices ginger, minced (or 1/4 teaspoon ground ginger)

    2 green onions, minced (or equal amount of Chinese chives, minced)

    4 teaspoons curry powder

    1 teaspoon salt

    3 tablespoons potato starch or cornstarch

    1 teaspoon *each* sesame oil and oil

    1 tablespoon oyster sauce

This filling may be prepared one or two days in advance and kept in refrigerator. If frozen, thaw before filling dumplings.

* Over-the-counter ground beef will not do justice for this recipe.

SPICY TURKEY FILLING 辣火雞餡　　火雞餡 TURKEY FILLING

Mix together:

1	lb. ground turkey
2/3	cup finely chopped celery (use only the tender parts)
1-1/2	tablespoons cornstarch
1/2	teaspoon salt
1	teaspoon chicken flavor stock base (powder bouillon)
2	to 3 teaspoons chili oil
1	teaspoon sesame oil
2	teaspoons teriyaki barbecue and marinade sauce
1	tablespoon tomato paste

For advance preparation, refrigerate or freeze filling.

Mix together:

1	package (about 1 lb.) ground turkey
1/4	cup minced water chestnuts
2	to 3 tablespoons minced green onion or Chinese chives
2	tablespoons cornstarch
1/8	teaspoon *each* ground ginger and pepper
1/2	teaspoon salt
1	teaspoon *each* sherry, oil and sesame oil
1	tablespoon soy sauce

Use as filling for *won ton*, *fun gor*, *shiu mai*, *pot stickers* or other dumplings. Or, steam (about 20 minutes) and serve over hot cooked rice. It is economical and low in calories.

Filling may be refrigerated or frozen.

VEGETARIAN FILLING PORK AND CABBAGE FILLING

1/2	lb. napa cabbage
1	to 1-1/2 tablespoons cornstarch
1/4	cup water
1	10-oz. can vegetarian abalone, minced
1	teaspoon soy sauce

pinch ground pepper

salt to taste

Blanch cabbage in boiling water until limp.
Drain, squeeze out excess liquid, then mince.
Cook mixture of cornstarch and water to a
thickened paste. Add cabbage, vegetarian
abalone, soy sauce, pepper and salt; mix well.

Use filling as soon as possible.

1/4	lb. napa cabbage
1	lb. ground pork, see ground pork, page 8
1/4	teaspoon ground pepper
3	tablespoons cornstarch
1/2	to 3/4 teaspoon salt
1	tablespoon *each* soy sauce and sherry
2	teaspoons *each* sesame oil and oil

Blanch cabbage in boiling water until limp. Drain,
squeeze out excess liquid, then chop finely (should
measure 1/2 cup). Add other ingredients; mix well.
For the pouch type of dumplings with an open top,
dice one link Chinese pork sausage, red or green
bell pepper, or salty duck egg yolks for garnish.

Use filling as soon as possible.

SPICY SHRIMP FILLING 辣蝦餡

Mix:

1/2	lb. cooked shrimp meat, diced
2	to 3 tablespoons minced coriander
1/4	teaspoon salt
1	teaspoon potato starch or cornstarch
1/4	teaspoon sugar
1-1/2	teaspoons prepared Chinese hot mustard
1/2	teaspoon sesame oil
1/2	teaspoon *each* chili oil and sherry

For advance preparation, refrigerate or freeze filling.

海鮮餡 CURRIED SEAFOOD FILLING

1/2	lb. cooked shelled diced shrimp or flaked crab meat
1/4	cup minced green onion
1/8	teaspoon chili powder
2	teaspoons curry powder
1/2	tablespoon sesame oil
1	tablespoon oil
1/2	cup minced tender part of celery

salt to taste

Mix:

1	tablespoon cornstarch
1/4	cup water

Stir-fry celery in hot oil for 2 minutes. Add cornstarch mixture; stir until thickened. Turn off heat. Add remaining ingredients; mix well.

Filling may be prepared in advance and refrigerated.

Sweet Dim Sum

CHINESE MAGIC PUFFS, page 89

SWEET DATE-NUT PASTRIES, page 99

CHINESE MAGIC PUFFS
makes 20

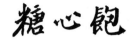

2 cans refrigerated extra-light buttermilk biscuit dough

4 blocks brown slab sugar, cut each in 3/4" small blocks, about 24 pieces

Honey Glaze: blend to obtain drizzling consistency

    1 cup sifted powdered sugar

    2 teaspoons honey

    4 teaspoons water

Separate dough into 20 pieces. Stretch a piece of dough to 1-1/2 times its original size. Place a sugar block in the center. Gather edges of dough to enclose, pinching and twisting to seal tightly. Place in greased mini muffin pan. Repeat until all puffs are made. Place muffin pans on oven liner; bake at 350° F. for 15 minutes or until golden brown. Remove puffs from pans at once. Drizzle with Honey Glaze. Serve hot.

VARIATION #1: Fill the hollow puffs with peanut butter, preserves or a sweet filling.

VARIATION #2: Prepare 1 recipe STEAMED BUN DOUGH. After the first rising, divide dough into 24

pieces. Melt 2/3 cup butter; mix 1/2 cup sugar with 1 teaspoon cinnamon; and have 24 large marshallows ready. Stretch a piece of dough to a 4" round. Dip a marshallow in butter, then roll in cinnamon-sugar. Place this coated marshallow in the center of the dough. Gather edges of dough to enclose marshallow and pinch to seal tightly. Place puff in buttered regular muffin pan. Cover with cloth. Repeat with remaining dough. Let rise until dough (not the whole puff) is almost doubled in bulk, about 30 minutes. Brush puffs with remaining melted butter. Place muffin pans on oven liner; bake at 350° F. for 15 minutes or until golden. Remove puffs from pans at once. Drizzle with glaze.

These magic puffs are children's favorite snacks. With the convenient refrigerated dough, they can make the puffs themselves.

FLAKY TART SHELLS
makes 10 to 12 tart shells

畳 撻 皮

Dough A:

  1/3 cup shortening

      pinch of salt

  1 large egg yolk

  1 cup all-purpose flour

  3 to 4 teaspoons ice cold water

Dough B:

  2 tablespoons softened butter

  1/2 cup cake flour (more if needed, see
      below)

To prepare dough A: In a small mixing bowl, stir shortening, salt and yolk until well blended. Add flour; do not stir. Place bowl in refrigerator to chill for 30 to 60 minutes. Blend ingredients with a pastry blender or two knives until fine. Add water, a teaspoon at a time, until mixture will hold together. Divide dough evenly into 10 to 12 (depending on size of tart pans) portions. Roll into balls. *DO NOT OVERWORK DOUGH.*

To prepare dough B: Blend flour and butter with two knives or pastry blender. The dough should be somewhat dry and crumbly. If the dough will hold together and have the consistency of pie dough, add 1 to 3 teaspoons cake flour; blend well. Divide dough into 10 to 12 portions.

Flatten a piece of dough A. Place a portion of dough B in the center and wrap around with dough A to form a ball. Place a ball between two sheets of lightly dusted waxed paper (only while rolling with pin) and roll it out to a 1/8" to 1/4" thick rectangle. Then, starting with a short side, roll up into a stick. Turn stick so that one end points toward you, and roll out into a rectangle of 1-1/2"x5". Starting with a narrow end, fold up to get a 4-layered square. Keep covered. Repeat until all squares are made.

Take a square of dough. Roll it (between two sheets of dusted waxed paper) out into 1/8" thickness. Cut a circle slightly larger than the inverted tart pan and lightly dust one side of the circle with flour. Loosely fit into tart pan with the dusted side down.

This enables the tart to slide out when cooked.

For advance preparation, wrap tart shells in plastic bags and refrigerate until ready to fill and bake. Dough A, by itself, makes an excellent 9" pie crust.

IMPORTANT: Always handle this type of dough as little as possible.

布丁撻   DESSERT TARTS
         10-12 tarts

1 recipe FLAKY TART SHELLS, page 90
ice cream or pudding

Make tart shells as directed. Prick crusts with fork. Bake at 350° F. until golden. Remove from oven; cool. Store tart shells in container or refrigerate. Fill shells just before serving.

VARIATION: Fill baked tart shells with any ready-to-eat sweet filling.

CHINESE CUSTARD TARTS
makes 10 to 12 tarts　　蛋　撻

1　recipe FLAKY TART SHELLS, page 90
Filling:

- 2　extra large eggs
- 6　tablespoons sugar
- 1/8　teaspoon salt
- 1　cup milk
- 1　teaspoon almond extract/imitation banana extract/vanilla

Prepare tart shells as directed and preheat oven to 325^0-350^0 F.

Beat eggs, sugar and salt just to blend. Add milk and extract; stir only to blend. Let it rest for 10 minutes. This helps to reduce the air bubbles beaten into the mixture. Pour mixture through a sieve. *Carefully* fill tart shells. Place custard tarts on a baking sheet and place baking sheet on the lower or lowest rack (depending on the size of the oven) of the oven so that the tarts are just below the center of the oven. Bake at 325^0-350^0 F. and check for doneness after 20 minutes. Baking time may take 20 to 30 minutes. Cool 10 minutes. Then turn tarts upside down to loosen, but do not remove from pans. Cool completely, then remove from tart pans and place in paper baking cups.

To make good custard tarts: Watch your oven temperature and your baking time closely. Oven temperatures vary. Over-baking can cause filling to become watery and toughen. Generally, custard is done when a knife inserted in center comes out clean, though it may be overcooked. The center "finishes cooking" after the custard is removed from heat. Therefore, the center should not be firmly set when the tarts are taken out of the oven. If the custard sets too fast and the crust is uncooked, place a second cookie sheet two racks above the tarts. Custard tarts are best when eaten fresh. Cooled tarts should be refrigerated.

The development of this recipe was a tremendous challenge. It took several trials to perfect this buttery flavored flaky dough, and several bakings to find the best baking method so that the crust is flaky and the custard is smooth and velvety. If your custard tarts turn out perfect the first time, congratulations! Otherwise, try it again. Perfection comes with practice. As the Chinese say, "Failure is the mother of success."

SWEET WON TON CRESCENTS 甜雲吞角
makes 3 dozen

糯粉皮 BASIC SWEET DOUGH

round won ton skins, see won ton skins, page 11
oil for deep-frying
Filling: mix

   1/2 cup shelled dry-roasted sunflower seeds
        (or raw sunflower seeds)

 1-1/2 cups shredded coconut

   1/2 cup finely chopped red & green cherries,
        pineapple or citron

 1-1/2 tablespoons soft butter

     2 tablespoons white corn syrup or honey

     2 tablespoons finely chopped crystalized
        ginger (or 2 more tablespoons of cherries,
        pineapple or citron)

Fill won ton skin with about 2 teaspoons filling.
Fold in half. Seal edges with a dab of water or
beaten egg. Proceed similarly with remaining filling. Deep-fry in 350^0 F. hot oil until evenly
golden. Drain on absorbent paper. Serve.

These sweet crescents will keep for a few days if
stored in closed container. Reheat in slow oven
to restore crispness, if needed.

2 cups glutinous rice flour (sweet rice flour)
6 tablespoons firmly packed brown sugar
10 tablespoons water
glutinous rice flour for dusting

Bring sugar and water to a boil. Quickly pour syrup
into flour while stirring to get a partially cooked
dough. Knead in bowl until smooth, adding more hot
water or flour as needed to make a workable dough.
Keep covered. Let rest for 5 minutes before shaping.

檸檬雲吞條

square won ton skins, see won ton skins, page 11
oil for deep-frying
Mix:

    1-1/2   teaspoons shake-on dry lemon juice or
             cinnamon

      1   cup sifted powdered sugar

Cut won ton skins into two equal rectangles. Take
one strip and cut 3 slits in the center, then pull
one end of the rectangle through the middle slit
to resemble a bow tie. Make as many as desired.
Deep-fry in 350° F. hot oil until evenly golden.
Drain on absorbent papers. Sprinkle with lemon-
sugar. Serve for snacks.

VARIATIONS: Try sprinkling the fried "bow ties"
with curry powder or powdered cheese.

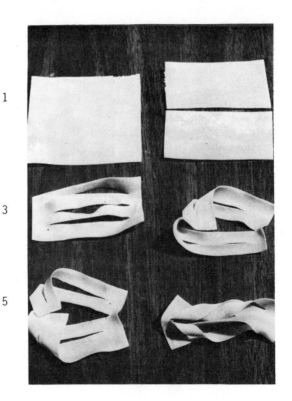

CHINESE APPLE PIES
makes 8

蘋果捲

paper-thin (not the won ton skin type) spring roll
skins
1 21-oz. can apple pie filling mixed with 1/2
teaspoon cinnamon
oil for deep-frying

Place a perfect (no cracks or tears) skin on counter
with a corner pointing toward you. Spoon 3 or 4
chunks of apple (very little sauce, please) over
skin about 2-1/2" from this corner. Fold this corner
over to cover filling. Roll over twice toward the
far corner. Fold in both side flaps. Fold the last
corner over to cover, tucking the tip of this last
corner in and under the side flaps. Place on flat
surface with seam side down. Repeat until all turnovers are made.

Heat oil to 375° F. Lower turnovers into hot oil
with chopsticks holding and keeping seams together
to prevent seams from popping open during the first
20 seconds or so. Deep-fry until golden, 1 to 1-1/2
minutes, rolling frequently. Drain on absorbent
toweling. Serve while crisp and hot.

MOON CAKES
makes 6 cakes   月 餅

Dough:
- 1-1/2 cups all-purpose flour
- 1/4 cup instant nonfat dry milk
- 1 teaspoon baking powder
- 1/8 teaspoon salt
- 1/4 cup brown sugar
- 1 large egg
- 1/2 stick (1/4 cup) butter or margarine, melted

Filling: mix together
- 1 cup coconut flakes
- 1 cup finely chopped walnuts
- 1 cup finely chopped dates
- 1 cup lotus nut paste or red bean paste
- 2 tablespoons softened butter

Mix:
- 1 egg yolk
- 1/2 teaspoon sesame oil

Grind dry milk in a blender or food processor to make the granules into a finer powder. Place flour, dry milk, baking powder and salt in a mixing bowl. Beat egg with sugar until sugar is dissolved. Gradually add egg mixture and butter to the dry ingredi-

ents. Mix well with 2 knives or pastry blender to get a dry dough similar to pie dough. Roll out the dough to about 1/16" thickness. Cut a piece of dough large enough to line the bottom and sides of the moon cake mold (or a tart pan). Gently press into place. Spread and press filling over dough, leaving enough room at the top for a layer of crust. Cut another piece of dough to cover the filling; gently press into place. Remove excess dough and return it to the bowl. Firmly but gently press all over the cake to get a good impression and smooth surface (this will be the bottom). Holding the mold, cake facing down, in one hand, give it a whack against a hard edge (such as the table edge or the center divider of the sink), catching the cake with the other hand as it is released from the mold. Place cake on baking sheet. Repeat until all cakes are made. Brush tops and sides with yolk mixture. Bake at 350° F. in the center of the oven until the bottom is golden brown, 18-22 minutes. Turn heat dial to broil. Open oven door partially and watch the cake tops turn brown, about 30 seconds or so. As soon as the tops have acquired the desired brown color, remove cakes from oven and transfer to racks to cool. Store in container at room temperature or refrigerate or freeze for longer period. Moon cakes are rich; cut into slices before serving.

VARIATIONS: There is an endless variety of moon cakes. Cakes can be filled with lotus nut paste, red bean paste, any sweet filling having a somewhat thick consistency, or even a filling with chips of preserved meat.

Moon cake plays the counterpart of CHEI JEI (page 138 in Lonnie Mock's *DIM SUM COOKBOOK*). It also symbolizes a happy occasion. Prior to the wedding, the groom's family presents a large quantity of these cakes (for this purpose, the cakes are simply called cakes, not moon cakes) to the bride's family who then distributes them among their friends and relatives.

Moon cake mold is hard to find and is very expensive. It is a beautiful piece of art work and can be used to decorate your kitchen. It is similar to the butter mold, having the approximate size of 3" to 3-1/4" in diameter and 1-1/4" deep.

Moon cakes were originated as a secret mission--so the story goes. Messages were hidden inside these giant cookies to summon the people to unite and fight against the Tartars. August 15th of the lunar calendar is the Mid-Autumn Festival. The moon shines brightest on this night. Friends and family members get together to admire the brilliance of the moon and to enjoy the bounty of their harvest. Chinese grapefruits, moon cakes and small taro roots are commonly offered to the goddess of the moon and then eaten by all (with joy!). During this period, moon cakes are given to friends as gifts, and served to guests who come to call. Mid-Autumn Festival is very much similar to Thanksgiving.

蓮蓉酥

1   recipe FLAKY BAKING PASTRY DOUGH, page 37
1   can sweetened lotus nut paste
Mix:

    1   egg yolk
    2   teaspoons water

Prepare dough as directed. Take a square of dough;
cut it in halves. Roll out each half into a 2-1/2"
to 3" round, giving the edges an extra pressing so
the center is thicker than the edge. Place 2 teaspoons filling on one circle; cover filling by
placing the second circle on top. Pinch edges together to seal tightly. Crimp sealed edge by holding the pastry between thumb and fingers of one
hand. Using sides of thumb and forefinger of the
other hand, pinch dough along edge of circle, fluting it as you would pie crust. Place on greased
baking sheet. Brush top with yolk mixture. Repeat
with remaining dough. Bake at 350° F. until golden,
25 to 30 minutes. Cool. Serve any time. If refrigerated, these pastries will keep for weeks.

SWEET DATE-NUT PASTRIES　甜棗酥　　綠豆餅　BEAN FLOUR COOKIES
makes 16　　　　　　　　　　　　　　　　makes 10 cookies

1　recipe FLAKY BAKING PASTRY DOUGH, page 37

Date-Nut Filling:　mix

    1　cup coconut flakes

    1　cup chopped walnuts

    1　cup finely chopped dates

    2　tablespoons softened butter

 1/4　cup light corn syrup

Mix:

    1　egg yolk

    2　teaspoons water

     few drops sesame oil

Prepare dough as directed. Roll out a piece of
dough into a 4" circle; dot the center with a
tablespoon filling. Gather edges and twist to
enclose filling securely. Flatten pastry slightly
and brush the smooth top with yolk mixture. Place
on lightly greased cookie sheet. Repeat until all
pastries are made. Bake at 350° F. until golden
brown, 25 to 30 minutes. Cool and store in a
container. For longer storage, refrigerate or
freeze.

4-1/2　tablespoons sugar

 3/4　cup green bean powder

   6　tablespoons all-purpose flour

   3　tablespoons almond powder

   3　tablespoons smooth peanut butter

 1/4　cup (1/2 stick) soft butter

 1/2　tablespoon light corn syrup

oil for brushing cookie mold, if needed

Blend ingredients with pastry blender until fine,
then work the crumbly dough with hand to mix well.
Lightly brush Chinese carved wooden cookie mold
with oil, if needed. Pack dough into mold, leveling off excess and pressing firmly to make dough
stick together and to get a good impression. Holding the mold, cookie side down, in one hand, give it
a gentle whack (once or twice) against a hard edge
(such as the table edge or the center divider of the
sink), catching the cookie with the other hand as it
drops off the mold. Put cookie on non-stick baking
sheet. Repeat until all cookies are made. Bake in
a 350° F. oven until the bottom is golden, about 15
minutes. Cool. Store in closed container.

FRIED RICE FLOUR COOKIES
makes 12 cookies

炒米餅

1-1/2 cups fried rice flour, see below
6 tablespoons sugar
6 tablespoons brown sugar
9 tablespoons butter or margarine, softened

To make fried rice flour: Purchase precooked packaged rice (such as Minute Rice). Fry rice in an ungreased wok until evenly golden, stirring constantly. Powder the fried rice in a blender (not the food processor); sift to obtain a fine powder. Place fried rice flour, sugars and butter in a mixing bowl. Work the ingredients with hand until well mixed. The dough is similar to brown sugar in texture. Fill an ungreased Chinese wooden cookie mold (cookie size is approximately 2-1/2" in diameter and 6/16" thick) with dough; press firmly to get a good impression, especially the edges. Hold the cookie mold with cookie side down, give it a whack against a hard edge (such as the table edge or the center divider of the sink), catching the cookie with the other hand as it is released from the mold. Place cookie on a smooth surface. Repeat until all cookies are made. Leave cookies out to dry and harden overnight. Store in closed container and

keep at room temperature. Serve any time.

If the Chinese cookie mold is not available, pack and mold two tablespoons of dough into a ball. Chinese villagers make these fried rice flour balls either very soft or very hard (jawbreakers). The hard balls will get harder as they age, and in time they will become very hard to bite (and break your teeth!) but that's why they are so good. As young children, we loved these jawbreakers as much as ice cream, and mother never made them often enough.

CRYSTAL COOKIES
makes 10 to 12 cookies
彩晶餅

Dough:

    1 cup wheat starch

  1/2 cup glutinous rice flour (sweet rice flour)

    5 tablespoons sugar

    6 to 6-1/2 tablespoons water

    2 tablespoons lard or shortening

1 can ready-to-use sweetened lotus nut paste

1 salted duck egg, see below

Scrape preserving material off egg. Rinse until clean. Shell and cut yolk into pea-sized pieces, reserving egg white for other uses. In a small saucepan, bring 6 tablespoons water and sugar to a boil. Place wheat starch and rice flour in a small mixing bowl. Pour boiling syrup into flour while stirring to form a dough. Stir well; let cool until dough is warm. Add lard and knead until the dough is smooth, adding more water (6-1/3 tablespoons is usually sufficient with most brands of flour) if necessary. The dough should be some-what soft but not too sticky. If the dough is too dry, the cookies will be hard and won't get cooked.

Oil a Chinese wooden cookie mold. Stretch a piece of dough to a 3" circle, thinning the edges more than the center. Dot the center with 1 tablespoon filling. Gather edges to enclose filling and roll into a smooth ball. Press ball into cookie mold to get a clear impression. (If Chinese wooden mold is not available, gently flatten the ball with hand.) Hold the cookie mold with cookie side down, give it a whack against a hard edge, catching the cookie with the other hand as it is released from the mold. Place cookie on lightly greased steaming tray. Garnish the top with a bit of yolk. Repeat until all cookies are made. Steam over high heat until done, about 20 minutes. When cooked and cooled, the cookies have a crystal or translucent look. If cookies are hard and white (the color of raw dough), they are not cooked through or the dough was too dry. Serve *hot.*

Refrigerated or frozen cookies should be steamed until soft before serving.

FLAKY STEAMED BUN DOUGH　　酥 飽 皮

Dough A:

  2-3/4 teaspoons or 1 packet active dry yeast

     1 cup warm water

   3/4 teaspoon salt

   1/2 cup sugar

     1 tablespoon melted shortening

  1-1/2 cups white rice flour

  2-1/2 cups all-purpose flour

      all-purpose flour for dusting (as little as possible)

Dough B:

   1/2 cup all-purpose flour

  2-1/2 tablespoons shortening or lard

To prepare dough A: Add a tablespoon of the measured sugar to the dry yeast; stir. Add water to yeast mixture; blend. When the yeast and sugar have dissolved completely, add shortening. Combine rice flour, all-purpose flour, salt and remaining sugar in a large bowl and stir a few times to mix. Gradually pour yeast mixture while stirring to form a dough. Let rest for 5 minutes. Turn out onto very lightly floured surface. Knead until smooth and elastic. Place dough in a greased bowl, cover with towel and let rise in warm place until dough is at least doubled (you should get almost one large mixing bowl full), 2 hours or longer. Punch down, cover and let rest a few minutes, then divide into 20 equal portions.

To prepare dough B: Mix ingredients with hand and knead until smooth. Divide into 20 equal portions.

Flatten a piece of dough A. Place a portion of dough B in the center and wrap around with dough A to form a ball. Roll out on lightly floured surface to a 1/4" thick rectangle. Then, starting with a short side, roll up into a stick. Turn stick so that one end points toward you, and roll out into a rectangle of approximately 1-1/2" by 6". Starting with a narrow end, fold up to get a 4-layered square. Keep covered. Repeat until all 20 squares are made. Now, the flaky steamed bun dough is ready to be rolled out into circles for filling.

LAYERED LOTUS BUNS 酥皮蓮蓉飽

makes 20 sweet buns

20 3-inch circular parchment papers
 1 recipe FLAKY STEAMED BUN DOUGH, page 102
 1 can sweetened lotus nut paste (or other
    sweet filling)
 5 salty duck egg yolks (optional), see below

Prepare dough as directed. Scrape preserving material off eggs; wash. Shell eggs, reserving egg whites for other uses. Wrap egg yolks in foil; bake at 350^0 F. for 15 minutes, then cut into quarters.

Roll out a square of dough into a 4" circle. Dot the center with 1 tablespoon filling and a piece of yolk. Bring edges together to enclose filling. Twist the gathered edges to insure a secure seal. Set bun, seam side down, on a piece of paper. Repeat until all buns are made. Arrange buns 2" apart on bamboo steamer, steaming trays or 10" cake racks. Cover with cloth and let rise in warm place until the dough is almost doubled in bulk, about 30 minutes. Steam over boiling water set on high heat for 12 to 15 minutes. Serve hot or cold.

Buns may be refrigerated or frozen. Reheat by steaming.

DOW SAH BAO
makes 20 sweet buns

豆沙飽　檸檬餅

LEMONY ALMOND COOKIES
makes 3 dozen

20   3-inch circular parchment papers
1   recipe STEAMED BUN DOUGH, page 31
1   can sweetened red bean paste

Prepare dough as directed. Flour hands. Shape dough evenly into two 10" long rolls. Cut rolls into 20 1-inch pieces. Stretch and shape each piece into a 4" circle. Fill with 1 tablespoon sweet paste. Bring round edges together to enclose filling. Twist the gathered edges to insure a secure seal. Set bun, seam side down, on a piece of paper. Arrange buns 2" apart on bamboo steamer, steaming trays or 10" cake racks. Cover with cloth and let rise until almost doubled in bulk, 10 to 20 minutes. Steam over boiling water (set on high heat) for 10 to 12 minutes. Serve hot or cold.

VARIATION: Fill buns with lotus nut paste. Salted duck egg yolk may be added in the center of the filling. Wrap egg yolks in foil; bake at 350° F. for 15 minutes, then place in the center of the filling whole, halved or quartered.

1/2   cup *each* soft butter and shortening
2   cups sifted powdered sugar
1   large egg
1   teaspoon almond extract
2   cups all-purpose flour
1/2   cup almond powder
1/2   teaspoon baking soda
1   teaspoon baking powder
Coating: mix
　　1-1/2   teaspoons shake-on dry lemon juice
　　1   cup sifted powdered sugar

Cream butter and shortening. Gradually cream in powdered sugar. Add egg and almond extract, continue beating until light and fluffy. Stir in almond powder. Stir together flour, baking soda and baking powder; add to creamed mixture and mix well. Chill dough for easier handling. Roll dough into walnut-sized balls; place on ungreased shallow pans or cookie sheets. Flatten balls to 1/4" to 1/3" thickness. Bake in 325° F. oven until delicately golden on the bottom, about 20 minutes. Cool. While slightly warm, roll in lemon-sugar. Cookies should be crisp and light.

Sauces and Dips

A large selection of sauces and dips are available at the Oriental food markets. Take a tour of Chinatown and explore new flavors. Sweet and sour sauce, sweet and sour duck sauce, ready-made **extra** hot mustard, hot sauce, chili oil, chili sauce, hot bean sauce, sweet bean sauce, plum sauce and subgum sauce are commonly displayed on the shelves. Find your favorite or create a sauce of your own.

GARLIC AND SOY DIP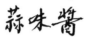

3   cloves garlic, finely minced
1/2 teaspoon sugar
2   tablespoons dark soy sauce
2   teaspoons oil

Heat oil until very hot. Add garlic and stir around a few times; do not brown. Mix in sugar and soy sauce; immediately remove from heat. Cool; pour into TOMATO BOWL, see FANCY GARNISHES. Serve with steamed dumplings, pan-fried foods, or meat.

薑汁醬 SWEET AND PUNGENT GINGER DIP

1   tablespoon finely minced ginger root
2   tablespoons brown sugar
2   teaspoons oil
3   tablespoons white vinegar
3   tablespoons tomato catsup
salt, if needed

Heat oil until hot; add ginger and stir a few times, do not brown. Add sugar, vinegar, catsup and salt (only if needed); stir until sugar is dissolved. Serve with pan-fried or deep-fried dumplings and meat.

CHILI OIL 辣油

1/4 to 1/3 cup salad oil
1 or 2 red chili peppers, depending on personal preference

Remove stems and seeds from peppers; pat dry. Heat oil until very hot but not smoking; add peppers and fry for about a minute. Remove from heat. Leave peppers in oil until the desired flavor is obtained.

辣蒜油 CHILI SESAME OIL

Substitute a small amount (or all) of sesame oil for salad oil in the CHILI OIL recipe.

SZECHWAN PEPPER SALT 花椒鹽

Toast Szechwan peppercorns in an ungreased pan for 3 to 5 minutes until brown, but not burned. Grind and sieve. Add to table salt in desired proportions (approximately 1 tablespoon pepper powder to 2 tablespoons salt). Store in jar at room temperature. Serve with deep-fried poultry dishes.

甜酸醬 SWEET AND SOUR SAUCE

2 teaspoons cornstarch
2 tablespoons brown sugar
1/8 teaspoon salt
2 tablespoons white vinegar
2 tablespoons catsup
1/4 cup water
2 teaspoons oil

Heat oil until hot. Add mixture of remaining ingredients; stir until thickened. Serve with fried foods.

Fancy Garnishes

ONION BRUSH 葱刷

蘿蔔輪 CARROT WHEELS OR CUCUMBER WHEELS

Use only the white part of the green onion. Cut a stalk 3" in length. Holding stalk vertically, make 1" to 1-1/4" vertical slashes 6 to 8 times at both ends. Soak in ice cold water and refrigerate until needed. The split ends will spring out into fringes.

Slice peeled carrot rounds or unpeeled cucumber rounds in 1/16" thickness, then cut nicks all the way around the slices.

番茄碗 TOMATO BOWL

ONION FLOWER 葱花

Cut the white part of a green onion in 3" length, then make several cuts two-thirds of the way down from one end. Soak in ice water and refrigerate until needed. The split ends will spring out into fringes.

Select a large firm-ripe tomato. Using a grapefruit knife, make zig zag cuts around the tomato between 1/4 & 1/3 of the way down from the stem end, cutting deeply into the center so that the top can be lifted off all in one piece. This top makes a perfect lid. Cut and spoon out the pulp and seeds, resulting in a hollowed tomato bowl. Fill bowl with dip or sauce. It makes a perfect garnish.

THE BUTTERFLY   蝴 蝶

Peel the big end of a large carrot. With a sharp thin narrow knife, cut 1 slice less than 1/16" (as thin as possible) thick. Do not slice through, leaving 1/4" to 1/3" uncut base. Cut a second slice, also less than 1/16" thick, slicing it through so now you have two slices connected together by the uncut base similar to the split hamburger bun in figure 1. Place carrot round flat on the table. Cut off a thin curved strip as shown, cutting through both slices thus resulting in 2 antennae as in figure 2. Next, make a cut as illustrated in figure 3. Leave this piece of art in the refrigerator until it is slightly wilted and soft. Push point A upward and inward toward the opposite side B (see photos on the left and in the center) until it rests between and on the uncut base in the center (see photo on the right). This gives the most beautiful three dimensional butterfly. Soak in cold water to restore freshness, then use for garnish. Congratulations! You have just created a masterpiece!

1

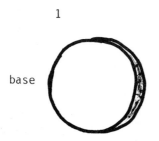

base

2

base

3

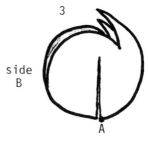

side
B

A

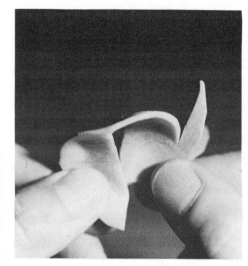

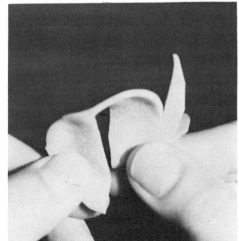

CUCUMBER ROSE 玫瑰

Slice (crosswise) unpeeled cucumber into 1/16" thickness. Cut round slices in halves. Starting with the small-est slices, arrange and bend slices around an imaginary central point, unpeeled green edges up, to resemble rose petals. Gradually overlap petals from the center of the rose to the largest outer petals. Arrange food pieces around the rose to support and keep the flower together. For a beautiful red rose, use a firm-ripe tomato.

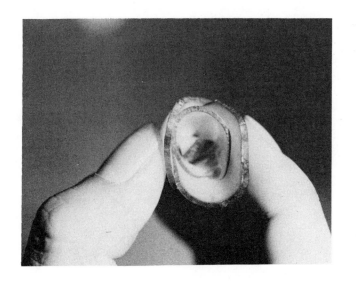

Suggested Menus

STUFFED PRAWNS, page 77

Below are seven suggested menus, one for each day of the week. Advance preparations are discussed in individual recipes. Each menu is carefully planned to provide harmony, contrast and variety. The work load is balanced. For example, a lengthy recipe is offset by a simple one, and last-minute cooking is reduced to a minimum. Cooking methods in each menu utilize the steamer, the skillet, the deep-fryer, the wok and/or the oven so that even if you decide to cook the entire meal at the last minute, you won't have to wash and wait for the same pan. Also, included in this section are two special groups of food to suit your particular interests.

MENU # I

      LUNCHEON for 3 or 4:

                    CHAR SHIU BAO or SHIU MAI or EGG SACK SHIU MAI
                    SHRIMP TOAST or HONEY-COMBED TARO CRESCENTS or CRISPY POTATO CRESCENTS
                    RED-COOKED DRUMSTICKS
                    LYCHEE TEA

         for 5 or 6, add:
                    RICE NOODLE ROLLS WITH SPICY BEEF FILLING
                    5-SPICED BISCUITS

MENU # II

      LUNCHEON for 3 or 4:

                    FUN GOR or TENDER CURRIED MEAT BALLS
                    POT STICKER PATTY CAKES or BEAN-CURD ROLLS
                    SHREDDED PORK CHOW MEIN
                    DRAGON'S WELL TEA

         for 5 or 6, add:
                    STUFFED PRAWNS or CHINESE SAUSAGE PANCAKES
                    SWEET RICE WITH CHICKEN WRAPPED IN LOTUS LEAF or SWEET DATE-NUT PASTRIES

MENU # III

    LUNCHEON for 3 or 4:

                FANCY FANS or HAR GOW

                PAN-FRIED PORK & SHRIMP PATTIES or GOLD COIN PORK

                BAKED CHAR SHIU BAO or FLAKY SWEET LOTUS TURNOVERS

                SILVER NEEDLES TEA

      for 5 or 6, add:

                POT STICKER ROLLS or POT STICKER TRIANGLES

                CHAR SHIU CHOW FUN or SUBGUM WAR MEIN

MENU # IV

    LUNCHEON for 3 or 4 (a vegetarian/seafood menu):

                VEGETARIAN SPRING ROLLS

                OYSTER FLAVORED ABALONE or DEEP-FRIED OYSTERS or SWEET AND SOUR PRAWNS

                CHINESE CUSTARD TARTS

                JASMINE TEA

      for 5 or 6, add:

                VEGETARIAN FUN GOR

                TEA EGGS

MENU # V

    LUNCHEON for 3 or 4 (a spicier menu):

                GARLICKY CHICKEN WINGS or CHAR SHIU SO

                ANTS CLIMBING TREE

                POT STICKERS (use CURRIED BEEF FILLING)

                OOLOONG TEA

      for 5 or 6, add:

                MO SHU PORK

                MANDARIN PANCAKES

MENU # VI

    WEEKEND DINNER (designed with children in mind):

                  SHRIMP ROLLS (as appetizer)

                  CHAR SHIU or PEPPER & STEAK CUBES

                  CRISP DEEP-FRIED DRUMSTICKS or RED DUCK

                  YANGCHOW FRIED RICE

                  CHINESE MAGIC PUFFS or LEMONY ALMOND COOKIES

MENU # VII

    WEEKEND DINNER (a spicier elegant menu):

                  GINGER BEEF ROLLS (as appetizer)

                  SIZZLING RICE SOUP

                  HOT & SPICY PRAWNS

                  CRISPY DUCK with CRESCENT SHAPED STEAMED BUNS

                  LEMONY WON TON TWISTS

For an impressive artistic "show", choose from this group:

CRYSTAL SHIU MAI	FUN GOR (crimped, of course!)
CHAR SHIU BAO (with pleated side up)	FUN GOR TORTELLINI
CHAR SHIU SO	HAR GOW
FOUR-COLORED SHIU MAI	FLOWERET SHIU MAI

For hors d'oeuvres, choose from this group:

GINGER BEEF ROLLS	POT STICKER TRIANGLES
EGG SACK SHIU MAI	SHIU MAI
FRIED CURRIED BEEF WON TON	SHRIMP ROLLS
POT STICKER ROLLS	SWEET WON TON CRESCENTS

RECIPE INDEX

NOTES

NOTES

EXCEL IN CHINESE COOKING

EXCEL IN CHINESE COOKING is a comprehensive volume of authentic recipes. This book covers a wide range of dishes--beef, pork, poultry, seafood, vegetables, noodles, rice, dim sum, desserts, sauces and dips. Other special features include: cutting techniques, Chinese-English shopping list, cooking methods, fancy garnishes and suggested menus. It provides a perfect balance for FAVORITE DIM SUM and 141½ CHINESE-STYLE CHICKEN RECIPES. All three volumes complement each other.

Some specific recipes are: Cantonese Roasted Pork, Sweet And Sour Pork, Melt-In-The-Mouth Steaks, Mongolian Beef, Szechwan Spicy Beef, Pressed Duck, Crisp And Savory Peking Duck, Crisp Tangy Lemon Chicken, Flavor-Potted Chicken, Low-Cal Chicken Meat, Stir-Fried Chicken In Wine Sauce, Char Shiu Fried Rice, Long Life Noodle Soup, Chinese Rice Tamales, Won Ton War Mein, Coiled Sausage Buns, Fried Fun Gor, Honey Char Shiu Bao, Honey Jerky, Sandwich Pockets, So Bao, Garlicky Hoisin Dip, Sweet And Sour Sauce, Crisp Aromatic Fish, Hot And Spicy Stir-Fried Prawns, Lobster Cantonese, Steamed Fish, Beef Asparagus, Beef With Plenty of Veggies, Poultry Stuffing, Stir-Fried Snow Peas With Prawns, Vegetarian Food, Pineapple Chicken Salad, and much more.

EXCEL IN CHINESE COOKING is written in the English language, fully illustrated with instructional photos and step-by-step sketches. Recipes have all been kitchen tested and tasted tested. The ultimate goal of EXCEL IN CHINESE COOKING is to give dependable recipes with precise directions so the family chef can create mouth-watering Chinese meals at home.

141 AND ONE-HALF CHINESE-STYLE CHICKEN RECIPES

141 AND ONE-HALF CHINESE-STYLE CHICKEN RECIPES is a handsome, complete, 208-page volume, composed of 143 recipes plus variations. There is a recipe to suit every taste bud and any occasion, from elaborate to informal. Recipes cover every aspect of dining: breakfast, brunch, dim sum luncheon, one-dish meals, entrees, elegant banquet specialties, midnight snacks, pre-dinner appetizers and in-between-meal snacks.

Chicken can be stir-fried, roasted, boiled, braised, deep-fried, steamed, poached, smoked, barbecued, and recipes sometimes utilize a combination of two different cooking techniques. Because recipes cover every aspect of dining and are so diversified in cooking methods, one can actually serve a three-course chicken dinner.

Other special features are: cutting up a chicken into parts, deboning chicken breast, skinning a whole fowl, deboning a whole fowl, and chopping a whole fowl into serving pieces and reassembling the pieces into the original form. A convenient Chinese shopping list is provided.

Some specific recipes are: Almond Chicken, Cashew Chicken With Vegetables, Chicken Over Sizzling Rice, Chicken With Asparagus, Chicken With Lemon Sauce, Chinese Chicken Salad, Crispy Chicken, Firepot Dinner, Hot And Sour Soup, Hot And Sour Chicken, Kung Pao Chicken, Mo Shu Chicken, Pineapple Chicken Delight, Roasted Soy Chicken, Roasted Turkey, Steamed Chicken In Black Bean Sauce, Stir-Fried Chicken (5 recipes), Stuffed Boneless Whole Chicken, Stuffed Boneless Chicken Wings, Velvety Chicken, Taro Rounds and others.

Chicken is nutritious, economical, versatile, low in cholesterol, low in fat, high in protein, but best of all, d-e-l-i-c-i-o-u-s!

ORDER FORM

NAME_____

NO. AND STREET_____

CITY_____

STATE_____

ZIP_____

ADDRESS ALL INQUIRIES & BOOK ORDERS

to

ALPHA GAMMA ARTS
P. O. BOX 4671
WALNUT CREEK, CALIFORNIA 94596-0671

description	quantity	unit price	postage & handling	total
FAVORITE DIM SUM		$4.95		
141 AND ONE-HALF CHINESE-STYLE CHICKEN RECIPES		$6.95		
EXCEL IN CHINESE COOKING		$7.95		

* For orders of 1 to 10 books, the rate is $1 for the first
    book. Add 40¢ per book up to 10 books. For larger orders,
    please write to us.